THE BLOOD *of* CHRIST – WHAT JESUS SAID

Inspired by the Holy Spirit

As assembled by

BERRY PEARSON

Copyright © 2021 Berry Pearson

All rights reserved. No part of this book may be reproduced, stored, or transmitted by any means—whether auditory, graphic, mechanical, or electronic—without written permission of both publisher and author, except in the case of brief excerpts used in critical articles and reviews. Unauthorized reproduction of any part of this work is illegal and is punishable by law.

ISBN: 978-1-63950-075-8 (sc)
ISBN: 978-1-63950-076-5 (e)

Because of the dynamic nature of the Internet, any web addresses or links contained in this book may have changed since publication and may no longer be valid. The views expressed in this work are solely those of the author and do not necessarily reflect the views of the publisher, and the publisher hereby disclaims any responsibility for them.

Writers Apex

Gateway Towards Success

8063 MADISON AVE #1252
Indianapolis, IN 46227
+13176596889
www.writersapex.com

SPECIAL THANKS TO:

My Wife

Jeremy Stewart

Amanda Jones

Catherine Wriddley

Pamela Allen

The **LORD** thy **GOD** will raise up unto thee a **PROPHET** from the midst of thee, of thy brethren, like unto me; unto **HIM** ye shall hearken;

I will raise them up a **PROPHET** from among their brethren, like unto thee, and will put **MY WORDS** in **HIS mouth**; and **HE shall speak** unto them all that **I shall command HIM**.

And it shall come to pass, that whosoever will not hearken unto **MY WORDS** which **HE shall speak** in **MY NAME**, **I** will require it of him.

For Moses truly said unto the fathers, A **PROPHET** shall the **LORD** your **GOD** raise up unto you of your brethren, like unto me; **HIM** shall ye hear in all things whatsoever **HE shall say** unto you.

And it shall come to pass, that every soul, which will not hear that **PROPHET**, shall be destroyed from among the people.

While he yet spake, behold, a **BRIGHT CLOUD** overshadowed them: and behold a **VOICE** out of the **CLOUD**, which said, This is **MY BELOVED SON**, in whom **I AM**, well pleased; **HEAR YE HIM**.

Deuteronomy 18:15, 18-19
Acts 3:22-23
Matthew 17:5

King James Version

Thomas Nelson Publishing

What JESUS Said

MATTHEW

3:15 Suffer now: for thus it becometh us to fulfil all righteousness.

4:4 It is written, Man shall not live by bread alone, but by every **WORD** that proceedeth out of the mouth of **GOD**.
4:7 It is written again, Thou shalt not tempt the **LORD** thy **GOD**.
4:10 Get thee hence, Satan: for it is written, Thou shalt worship the **LORD** thy **GOD**, and **HIM** only shalt thou serve.
4:17 Repent: for the **Kingdom of Heaven** is at hand.
4:19 Follow **ME**, and **I** will make you fishers of men.

5:3 Blessed the poor in spirit: for theirs is the **Kingdom of Heaven**. 4 Blessed they that mourn: for they shall be comforted. 5 Blessed the meek: for they shall inherit the Earth. 6 Blessed they which do hunger and thirst after righteousness: for they shall be filled. 7 Blessed the merciful: for they shall obtain mercy. 8 Blessed the pure in heart: for they shall see **GOD**. 9 Blessed the peacemakers: for they shall be called the children of **GOD**. 10 Blessed they which are persecuted for righteousness sake: for theirs is the **Kingdom of Heaven**. 11 Blessed ye, when men shall revile you, and persecute, and shall say all manner of evil against you falsely, for **MY** sake. 12 Rejoice and be exceeding glad: for great your reward in **Heaven**: for so persecuted they the prophets which were before you. 13 Ye are the salt of the Earth. But if the salt have lost his savor, where with shall it be salted? it is thenceforth good for nothing, but to be cast out, and to be trodden under foot of men. 14 Ye are the light of the world. A city that is set on a hill cannot be hid. 15 Neither do men light a candle, and put it under a bushel, but on a candlestick, and it giveth light unto all that are in the house. 16 Let your light so shine before men, that they may see your good works, and glorify your **FATHER** which is in **Heaven**. 17 Think not that **I AM** come to destroy the law, or the prophets: **I AM** not come to destroy, but to fulfill. 18 For verily **I** say unto you, Till Heaven and Earth pass, one jot or one tittle shall in no wise pass from the law, till all be fulfilled. 19 Whosoever therefore shall break one of these least commandments, and teach men so, he shall be called the least in the **Kingdom of Heaven**: but whosover shall do and teach, the same shall be called great in the **Kingdom of Heaven**. 20 For **I** say unto you, That except your righteousness shall exceed of the scribes and Pharisees, ye shall in no case enter into the **Kingdom of Heaven.** 21 Ye have heard that it was said by them of old time. Thou shalt not kill; and whosoever shall kill shall be in danger of the judgement. 22 But **I** say unto you, That whosoever is angry with his brother without a cause shall be in danger of the judgement: and whosoever shall say to his brother, Raca, shall be in danger of the council: but whosoever shall say, Thou fool, shall be in danger of hell fire. 23 Therefore if thou bring thy gift to the altar, and there rememberest that thy brother hath aught against thee; 24 Leave there thy gift before the altar, and go thy way; first be reconciled to thy brother, and then come and offer thy gift. 25 Agree with thy adversary quickly, whiles thou art in the way with him; lest at any time the adversary deliver thee to the judge, and the judge deliver thee to the officer, and thou be cast into prison. 26 Verily **I** say unto thee, Thou shalt by no means come out thence, till thou hast paid the uttermost farthing. 27 Ye have heard that it was said by them of old time, Thou shalt not commit adultery: 28 But **I** say unto you, That whosoever looketh on a woman to lust after her hath committed adultery with her already in his heart. 29 And if thy right eye offend thee, pluck it out, and cast from thee: for it is profitable for thee that one of thy members should perish, and not thy whole body should be cast into hell. 30 And if thy right hand offend thee, cut it off, and cast from thee: for it is profitable for thee that one of thy members should perish, and not thy whole body should be cast into hell. 31 It hath been said, Whosoever shall put away his wife, let him give her a writing of divorcement: 32 But **I** say unto you, That whosoever shall put away his wife saving for the cause of fornication, causeth her to commit adultery: and whosoever shall marry her that is divorced committeth adultery. 33 Again, ye have heard that it hath been said by them of old time, Thou shalt not forswear thyself, but shalt perform unto the **LORD** thine oaths. 34 But **I** say unto you, Swear not at all; neither by Heaven; for it is GOD's throne: 35 Nor by the Earth; for it is **HIS** footstool: neither by Jerusalem; for it is the city of the **GREAT KING.** 36 Neither shalt thou swear by thy head, because thou canst not make one hair white or black. 37 But let your communication be, Yea, yea; Nay, nay: for whatsoever is more than these cometh of evil. 38 Ye have heard that it hath been said, An eye for an eye, and a tooth for a tooth: 39 But **I** say unto you, That ye resist not evil: but whosoever shall smite thee on thy right cheek, turn to him the other also. 40 And if any man will sue thee at law, and take away thy coat, let him have cloak also. 41 And whosoever shall compel thee to go a mile, go with him twain. 42 Give to him that asketh thee, and from him that would borrow of thee turn not thou away. 43 Ye have heard that it hath been said, Thou shalt love thy neighbour; and hate thine enemy. 44 But **I** say unto you, Love your enemies; Bless them that curse you, do good to them that hate you, and pray for them which despitefully use you, and persecute you; 45 That ye may be the children of your **FATHER** which is in **Heaven**: for **HE** maketh **HIS** sun to rise on the evil and on the good, and sendeth rain on the just and on the unjust. 46 For if ye love them which love you, what reward have ye? do not even the publicans the same? 47 And if ye salute your brethren only, what do ye more? do not even the publicans so? 48 Be ye therefore perfect, even as your **FATHER** which is in **Heaven is Perfect.**

6:1 Take heed that ye do not your alms before men, to be seen of them: otherwise ye have no reward of your **FATHER** which is in **Heaven** . 2 Therefore when thou doest alms, do not sound a trumpet before thee, as the hypocrites do in the synagogues and in the streets, that they may have glory of men. Verily **I** say unto you, They have their reward. 3 But when thou doest alms, let not thy left hand know what thy right hand doeth: 4 That thine alms may be in secret: and thy **FATHER** which seeth in secret **HIMSELF** shall reward thee openly. 5 And when thou prayest, thou shalt not be as the hypocrites: for they love to pray standing in the synagogues and in the corners of the streets, that they may be seen of men.Verily, **I** say unto you, They have their reward. 6 But thou, when thou prayest, enter into thy closet, and when thou hast shut thy door, pray to thy **FATHER** which is in secret; and thy **FATHER** which seeth in secret shall reward thee openly. 7 But when ye pray, use not vain repetitions, as the heathen: for they think that they shall be heard for their much speaking. 8 Be not ye therefore like unto them: for your **FATHER** knoweth what things ye have need of, before ye ask

HIM. 9 After this manner therefore pray ye: Our **FATHER** which art in **Heaven**, **HALLOWED** be **THY NAME**, 10 **THY KINGDOM** come. **THY WILL** be done in Earth as in **Heaven**. 11 Give us this day our daily bread. 12 And forgive us our debts, as we forgive our debtors, 13 And lead us not into temptation, but deliver us from evil; for **THINE** is the **KINGDOM**, and the **POWER**, and the **GLORY**, **FOR EVER, AMEN.** 14 For if ye forgive men their trespasses, your **HEAVENLY FATHER** will also forgive you. 15 But if ye forgive not men their trespasses, neither will your **FATHER** forgive your trespasses. 16 Moreover when ye fast, be not, as the hypocrites, of a sad countenance: for they disfigure their faces, that they may appear unto men to fast. Verily **I** say unto you. They have their reward. 17 But thou, when thou fastest, anoint thine head, and wash thy face; 18 That thou appear not unto men to fast; but unto thy **FATHER** which is in secret: and thy **FATHER,** which seeth in secret, shall reward thee openly. 19 Lay not up for yourselves treasures upon Earth, where moth and rust doth corrupt, and where thieves break through and steal: 20 But lay up for yourselves treasures in **Heaven**, where neither moth nor rust doth corrupt, where thieves do not break through nor steal: 21 For where your treasure is, there will your heart be also. 22 The light of the body is the eye: if therefore thine eye be single, thy whole body shall be full of light. 23 But if thine eye be evil, thy whole body shall be full of darkness. If therefore the light that is in thee be darkness, how great that darkness! 24 No man can serve two masters: for either he will hate the one, and love the other; or else he will hold to the one, and despise the other. Ye cannot serve **GOD** and mammon. 25 Therefore **I** say unto you, Take no thought for your life, what ye shall eat, or what ye shall drink; nor yet for your body, what ye shall put on. Is not the life more than meat, and the body than raiment? 26 Behold the fowls of the air: for they sow not, neither do they reap; nor gather into barns; yet your **Heavenly FATHER** feedeth them. Are ye not much better than they? 27 Which of you by taking thought can add one cubit unto his stature? 28 And why take ye thought for raiment? Consider the lilies of the field, how they grow; they toil not, neither do they spin: 29 And yet **I** say unto you, That even Solomon in all his glory was not arrayed like one of these. 30 Wherefore, if **GOD** so clothe the grass of the field, which today is, and tomorrow is cast into the oven, not much more you, O ye of little faith? 31 Therefore take no thought, saying, What shall we eat? or, What shall we drink? or, Wherewithal shall we be clothed? 32 (For after all these things do the Gentiles seek:) for your **Heavenly FATHER** knoweth that ye have need of all these things. 33 But seek ye first the **Kingdom of GOD**, and **HIS RIGHTEOUSNESS**: and all these things shall be added unto you. 34 Take therefore no thought for the morrow: for the morrow shall take thought for the things of itself. Sufficient unto the day the evil thereof.

7:1 Judge not, that ye be not judged. 2 For with what judgement ye judge, ye shall be judged: and with what measure ye mete, it shall be measured to you again. 3 And why beholdest thou the mote that is in thy brother's eye, but considerest not the beam that is in thine own eye? 4 Or how wilt thou say to thy brother, Let me pull out the mote out of thine eye; and, behold, a beam in thine own eye? 5 Thou hypocrite, first cast out the beam out of thine own eye: and then shalt thou see clearly to cast out the mote out of thy brother's eye. 6 Give not that which is holy unto the dogs, neither cast ye your pearls before swine, lest they trample them under their feet, and turn again and rend you. 7 Ask, and it shall be given you, seek, and ye shall find; knock, and it shall be opened unto you: 8 For every one that asketh receiveth; and he that seeketh findeth, and to him that knocketh it shall be opened. 9 Or what man is there of you, whom if his son ask bread, will he give him a stone? 10 Or if he ask a fish, will he give him a serpent? 11 If ye then, being evil, know how to give good gifts unto your children, how much more shall your **FATHER** which is in **Heaven** give good things to them that ask **HIM**? 12 Therefore all things whatsoever ye would that men should do to you, do ye even so to them: for this is the law and the prophets. 13 Enter ye in at the strait gate: for wide the gate; and broad the way, that leadeth to destruction, and many there be which go in thereat: 14 Because strait the gate, and narrow the way, which leadeth unto life, and few there be that find it. 15 Beware of false prophets, which come to you in sheep's clothing, but inwardly they are ravening wolves. 16 Ye shall know them by their fruits. Do men gather grapes of thorns, or figs of thistles? 17

Even so every good tree bringeth forth good fruit; but a corrupt tree bringeth forth evil fruit. 18 A good tree cannot bring forth evil fruit, neither a corrupt tree bring forth good fruit. 19 Every tree that bringeth not forth good fruit is hewn down, and cast into fire. 20 Wherefore by their fruits ye shall know them. 21 Not every one that saith unto **ME, LORD, LORD,** shall enter into the **Kingdom of Heaven**; but he that doeth the **WILL** of **MY FATHER** which is in Heaven. 22 Many will say to **ME** in that day, **LORD, LORD,** have we not prophesied in **THY NAME**? and in **THY NAME** have cast out devils? and in **THY NAME** done many wonderful works? 23 And then will **I** profess unto them, **I** never knew you: depart from **ME**, ye that work iniquity. 24 Therefore whosoever heareth these **SAYINGS** of **MINE**, and doeth **THEM**, **I** will liken him unto a wise man, which built his house upon a **ROCK**. 25 And the rain descended, and the floods came, and the winds blew, and beat upon that house; and it fell not: for it was founded upon a **ROCK**. 26 And every one that heareth these **SAYINGS** of **MINE**, and doeth **THEM** not, shall be likened unto a foolish man, which built his house upon the sand. 27 And the rain descended, and the floods came, and the winds blew, and beat upon that house, and it fell: and great was the fall of it.

8:3 I will, be thou clean. 4 See thou tell no man; but go thy way, show thyself to the priest, and offer the gift that Moses commanded for a testimony unto them.
8:7 I will come and heal him.
8:10 Verily **I** say unto you, **I** have not found so great faith, no, not in Israel. 11 And **I** say unto you, That many shall come from the east and the west, and shall sit down with Abraham, and Isaac, and Jacob, in the **Kingdom of Heaven**. 12 But the children of the **Kingdom** shall be cast into outer darkness: there shall be weeping and gnashing of teeth. 13 Go thy way, and as thou hast believed, be it done unto thee.
8:20 The foxes have holes, and the birds of the air nests; but the **SON** of **MAN** hath not where to lay head.
8:22 Follow **ME**, and let the dead bury their dead.
8:26 Why are ye fearful, O ye of little faith?

9:2 Son, be of good cheer; thy sins be forgiven thee.
9:4 Wherefore think ye evil in your hearts? 5 For whether is easier,to say, sins be forgiven thee, or to say, Arise, and walk? 6 But that ye may know that the **SON of MAN** hath **POWER** on Earth to forgive sins, Arise, take up thy bed, and go unto thine house.
9:9 Follow **ME**.
9:12 They that be whole need not a physician, but they that are sick. 13 But go ye and learn what that meaneth, **I** will have mercy, and not sacrifice: for **I AM** not come to call the righteous, but sinners to repentance.
9:15 Can the children of the bride-chamber mourn, as long as the **BRIDEGROOM** is with them? but the days will come, when the **BRIDEGROOM** shall be taken from them, and then shall they fast. 16 No man putteth a piece of new cloth unto old garment, for that which is put into fill it up taketh from the garment, and the rent is made worse. 17 Neither do men put new wine into old bottles: else the bottles break, and the wine runneth out, and the bottles perish: but they put new wine into new bottles, and both are preserved.
9:22 Daughter, be of good comfort; thy faith hath made thee whole.
9:24 Give place: for the maid is not dead, but sleepeth.
9:28 Believe ye that **I AM** able to do this? 29 According to your faith be it unto you. 30 See no man know.
9:37 The harvest truly plenteous, but the labourers few; 38 Pray ye therefore the **LORD** of the **Harvest**, that **HE** will send forth labourers into **HIS Harvest**.

10:5 Go not into the way of the Gentiles, and into city of the Samaritans enter ye not. 6 But go rather to the lost sheep of the house of Israel. 7 And as ye go, preach, saying, The **Kingdom of Heaven** is at hand. 8 Heal the sick, cleanse the lepers,raise the dead, cast out devils: freely ye have received, freely give. 9 Provide neither gold, nor silver, nor brass in your purses. 10 Nor scrip for your journey, neither two coats, neither shoes, nor yet staves: for the workman is worthy of his meat. 11 And into whatsoever city or town ye shall enter, inquire who in it is worthy: and there abide till ye go thence. 12 And when ye come into a house;

salute it. 13 And if the house be worthy, let your peace come upon it: but if it be not worthy, let your peace return to you. 14 And whosoever shall not receive you, nor hear your words, when ye depart of that house or city, shake off the dust of your feet. 15 Verily I say unto you, It shall be more tolerable for the land of Sodom and Gomorrah in the day of judgment, than for that city. 16 Behold, I send you forth as sheep in the midst of wolves: be ye therefore wise as serpents, and harmless as doves. 17 But beware of men: for they will deliver you up to the councils, and they will scourge you in their synagogues; 18 And ye shall be brought before governors and kings for **MY** sake, for a testimony against them and the Gentiles. 19 But when they deliver you up, take no thought how or what ye shall speak: for it shall be given you in that same hour what ye shall speak. 20 For it is not ye that speak; but the **SPIRIT** of your **FATHER** which speaketh in you. 21 And the brother shall deliver up the brother to death, and the father the child: and the children shall rise up against parents, and cause them to be put to death. 22 And ye shall be hated of all for **MY NAME's** sake: but he that endureth to the end shall be saved. 23 But when they persecute you in this city, flee ye into another: for verily I say unto you, Ye shall not have gone over the cities of Israel, till the **SON** of **MAN** be come. 24 The disciple is not above master, nor the servant above his lord. 25 It is enough for the disciple that he be as his master, and the servant as his lord. If they have called the **MASTER of the House** Beelzebub, how much more them of **HIS** household? 26 Fear them not therefore: for there is nothing covered, that shall not be revealed; and hid, that shall not be known. 27 What I tell you in darkness speak ye in light: and what you hear in the ear, preach ye upon the house tops. 28 And fear not them which kill the body, but are not able to kill the soul: but rather fear **HIM** which is able to destroy both soul and body in hell. 29 Are not two sparrows sold for a farthing? and one of them shall not fall on the ground without your **FATHER**. 30 But the very hair of your head are all numbered. 31 Fear ye not therefore, ye are of more value than many sparrows. 32 Whosoever therefore shall confess **ME** before men, him will I also confess before **MY FATHER** which is in **Heaven**. 33 But whosoever shall deny **ME** before men, him will I also deny before **MY FATHER** which is in **Heaven**. 34 Think not that **I AM** come to send peace on

The Blood of Christ

the Earth: **I** came not to send peace, but a sword. 35 For **I AM** come to set a man at variance against his father, and the daughter against her mother, and the daughter-in-law against her mother-in-law. 36 And a man's foes they of his own household. 37 He that loveth father or mother more than **ME** is not worthy of **ME**: and he that loveth son or daughter more than **ME** is not worthy of **ME**. 38 And he that taketh not his cross, and followeth after **ME**, is not worthy of **ME**. 39 He that findeth his life shall lose it: and he that loseth his life for **MY** sake shall find it. 40 He that receiveth you receiveth **ME**, and he that receive **ME** receiveth **HIM** that sent **ME**. 41 He that receiveth a prophet in the name of a prophet shall receive a prophet's reward; and he that receiveth a righteous man in the name of a righteous man shall receive a righteous man's reward. 42 And whosoever shall give to drink unto one of these little one's a cup of cold only in the name of a disciple, verily **I** say unto you, he shall in no wise lose his reward.

11:4 Go and show John again those things which ye do hear and see: 5 The blind receive their sight, and the lame walk, the lepers are cleansed, and the deaf hear, the dead is raised up, the poor have the gospel preached to them. 6 And blessed is, whosoever shall not be offended in **ME**. 7 What went ye out into the wilderness to see? A reed shaken with the wind? 8 But what ye out for to see? A man clothed in soft raiment? behold, they that wear soft are in king's houses. 9 But what went ye out for to see? A prophet? yea, **I** say unto you, and more than a prophet. 10 For this is, of whom it was written, Behold, **I** send **MY** messenger before **THY** face, which shall prepare **THY** way before **THEE**. 11 Verily, **I** say unto you, Among them that is born of women there hath not risen a greater than John the Baptist: notwithstanding he that is least in the **Kingdom of Heaven** is greater than he. 12 And from the days of John the Baptist until now the **Kingdom of Heaven** suffereth violence, and the violent take it by force. 13 For all the prophets and the law prophesied until John. 14 And if you will receive, this is Elias, which was for to come. 15 He that hath ears to hear, let him hear. 16 But whereunto shall **I** liken this generation? It is like unto children sitting in the markets, and calling unto their fellows. 17 And saying, We have piped unto you, and ye have not danced: we have mourned unto you, and ye have not lamented: 18 For John came neither eating or drinking, and they say, He hath a devil. 19 The **SON of MAN** came eating and drinking, and they say, Behold a **MAN** gluttonous, and a winebibber, a friend of publicans and sinners. But wisdom is justified of her children. **11:21** Woe unto thee, Chorazin! woe until you Bethsaida! for if the mighty works, which were done in you, had been done in Tyre and Sidon, they would have repented long ago in sackcloth and ashes. 22 But **I** say unto you, It shall be more tolerable for Tyre and Sidon at the day of judgment, than for you. 23 And thou, Capernaum, which art exalted **unto Heaven**, shalt be brought down to hell: for if the mighty works, which have been done in thee, have been done in Sodom, it would have remained until this day. 24 But **I** say unto you, That it shall be more tolerable for the land of Sodom in the day of judgment, than for thee. 25 **I** thank **THEE O FATHER, LORD of Heaven and Earth**, because **THOU** hast hid these things from the wise and prudent, and hast revealed them unto babes. 26 Even so, **FATHER**: for so it seemed good in **THY** sight. 27 All things are delivered unto **ME** of **MY FATHER**: and no man knoweth the **SON**, but the **FATHER**; neither knoweth any man the **FATHER**, save the **SON**, and to whomever the **SON** will reveal. 28 Come unto **ME**, all ye that labour and are heavy laden, and **I** will give you rest. 29 Take **MY** yoke upon you, and learn of **ME**; for **I AM MEEK** and **LOWLY in HEART**: and shall find rest unto your souls. 30 For **MY YOKE EASY**, and **MY BURDEN is LIGHT**.

12:3 Have ye not read what David did, when he was a hungered, and they that were with him; 4 How he entered into the **House of GOD**, and did eat the showbread, which was not lawful for him to eat, neither for them which were with him, but only for the priests? 5 Or have ye not read in the law, how that on the sabbath days the priests in the temple profane the sabbath, and are blameless? 6 But I say unto you, That in this place is greater than the temple. 7 But if ye have known what meaneth, **I** will have mercy, and not sacrifice, ye would not have condemned the guiltless. 8 For the **SON of MAN** is **LORD** even of the sabbath day.

The Blood of Christ

12:11 What man shall there be among you, that shall have one sheep, and it fall into a pit on the sabbath day, will he not lay hold of it, and lift out? 12 How much than is a man better than a sheep? Wherefore it is lawful to do well on the sabbath days. 13 Stretch forth thine hand.
12:25 Every kingdom divided against itself is brought to desolation; and every city or house divided against itself shall not stand: 26 And if Satan cast out Satan, he is divided against himself, how shall then his kingdom stand? 27 And if **I** by Beelzebub cast out devils, by whom do your children cast out? therefore they shall be your judges. 28 But if **I** cast out devils by the **SPIRIT of GOD**, then the **Kingdom of GOD** is come unto you. 29 Or else how can one enter into a strong man's house, and spoil his goods, except he first bind the strong man? And then he will spoil his house. 30 He that is not with **ME** is against **ME**; and he that gathered not with **ME** scattereth abroad. 31 Wherefore **I** say unto you, All manner of sin and blasphemy shall be forgiven unto men: but the blasphemy the **GHOST** shall not be forgiven unto men. 32 And whosoever speaketh a word against the **SON of MAN**, it shall be forgiven him: but whosoever speaketh against the **HOLY GHOST**, it shall never be forgiven him, neither in this world, neither in the to come. 33 Either make the tree good, and his fruit good; or else make the tree corrupt, and his fruit corrupt; for the tree is known by fruit. 34 O generation of vipers, how can ye, being evil speak good things? for out of the abundance of the heart the mouth speaketh. 35 A good man out of the good treasure of the heart bringeth forth good things: and an evil man out of the evil treasure bringeth forth evil things. 36 But, I say unto you, That every idle word that man shall speak, they shall give account thereof in the day of judgment. 37 For by thy words thou shalt be justified, and by thy words thou shalt be condemned.
12:39 An evil and adulterous generation seeketh after a sign; and there shall no sign be given to it, but the sign of the prophet Jonas: 40 For as Jonas was three days and three nights in the whale's belly; so shall the **SON of MAN** be three days and three nights in the heart of the Earth. 41 The men of Nineveh shall rise in judgement with this generation, and shall condemn it: because they repented at the preaching of Jonas; and, behold, **A GREATER** than Jonas is here. 42 The queen of the south shall rise up in judgement with this generation, and shall condemn it:

for she came from the uttermost parts of the Earth to hear the wisdom of Solomon; and, behold, **A GREATER** than Solomon here. 43 When an unclean spirit is gone out of a man, he walketh through dry places, seeking rest, and findeth none. 44 Then he saith, I will return into my house from whence I came out; and when he is come, he findeth empty, swept, and garnished. 45 Then goeth he, and taketh with himself seven other spirits more wicked than himself, and they enter in and dwell there; and the last of the man is worse than the first. Even so shall it be also unto this wicked generation. **12:48** Who is **MY** mother? and who are **MY** brethren? 49 Behold **MY** mother and **MY** brethren! 50 For whosoever shall do the will of **MY FATHER** which is in **Heaven**, the same is **MY** brother, and sister, and mother.

13:3 Behold, a sower went forth to sow; 4 And when he sowed, some fell by the wayside, and the fowls came and devoured them up: 5 Some fell upon stony places, where they had not much earth: and forthwith they sprung up, because they had no deepness of earth. 6 And when the sun was up, they scorched; and because they had no root, they withered away. 7 And some fell upon thorns, and the thorns sprung up, and choked them: 8 But other fell into good ground, and brought forth fruit, some an hundredfold, some sixtyfold, some thirtyfold. 9 Who hath ears to hear, let him hear.
13:11 Because it is given unto you to know the mysteries of the **Kingdom of Heaven**, but to them it is not given. 12 For whosoever hath, to him shall be given, and he shall have more abundance: but whosoever hath not, from him shall be taken away even that he hath.13 Therefore speak **I** to them in parables: because they seeing see not; and hearing they hear not, neither do they understand. 14 And in them is fulfilled the prophecy of Esaias, which saith, By hearing ye shall not hear, and shall not understand; and seeing ye shall see, and shall not perceive: 15 For this people's heart is waxed gross, and ears are dull of hearing, and their eyes they have closed; lest at any time they should see with eyes, and hear with ears, and should understand with heart, and should be converted, and **I** should heal them. 16 But blessed your eyes, for they see: and your ears, for they hear. 17 For verily **I** say unto you,

That many prophets and righteous have desired to see which ye see, and have not seen; and to hear which ye hear, and have not heard. 18 Hear ye therefore the parable of the sower. 19 When any one heareth the **WORD of the Kingdom**, and understandeth not, then come the wicked, and catcheth away that which was sown in his heart. This is he which received seed by the wayside. 20 But he that received the seed in stony places, the same is he that heareth the **WORD**, and anon with joy received it; 21 Yet hath he not root in himself, but dureth for a while: for when tribulation or persecution ariseth because of the **WORD**, by and by he is offended. 22 He also that received seed among the thorns is he that heareth the **WORD**; and the cares of this world, and the deceitfulness of riches, choke the **WORD**, and he becometh unfruitful. 23 But he that received the seed into the good ground is he that heareth the **WORD**, and understandeth; which also beareth fruit, and bringeth forth, some a hundredfold, some sixty, some thirty. 24 The **Kingdom of Heaven** is likened unto a man which sowed good seed in his field: 25 But while men slept, his enemy came and sowed tares among the wheat, and went his way. 26 But when the blade was sprung up, and brought forth fruit, then appeared the tares also. 27 So the servants of the householder came and said unto him, Sir, didst not thou sow good seed in the field? from whence then hath it tares? 28 He said unto them, An enemy hath done this. The servants said unto him, Wilt thou then that we go and gather them up? 29 But he said, Nay, lest while you gather up the tares, ye root up also the wheat with them. 30 Let both grow together until the harvest: and in the time of harvest I will say to the reapers, Gather ye together first the tares, and bind them in bundles to burn them: but gather the wheat into my barn. 31The **Kingdom of Heaven** is like unto a grain of mustard seed, which a man took, and sowed in his field: 32 Which indeed is the least of all seeds; but when it is grown, it is the greatest among herbs, and becometh a tree, so that the birds of the air come and lodge in the branches thereof. 33 The **Kingdom of Heaven** is like unto leaven, which a woman took, and hid in three measures of meal, till the whole was leavened.
13:37 He that sowed the good seed is the **SON of MAN**; 38 The field is the world: the good seed is the children of the **Kingdom**; but the tares are the children of the wicked one; 39 The enemy that sowed

them is the devil; the harvest is the end of the world; and the reapers are the angels. 40 As therefore the tares are gathered and burned in the fire; so shall it be in the end of the world. 41 The **SON of MAN** shall send forth **HIS** angels, and they shall gather out of **HIS Kingdom** all things that offend, and them which do iniquity; 42 And shall cast them into a furnace of fire: there shall be wailing and gnashing of teeth. 43 Then shall the righteous shine forth as the sun in the **Kingdom** of their **FATHER**. Who hath ears to hear, let him hear. 44 Again, the **Kingdom of Heaven** is like unto a treasure hid in a field; the which when a man hath found, he hideth, and for joy thereof goeth and selleth all that he hath, and buyeth that field. 45 Again, the **Kingdom of Heaven** is like unto a merchant man, seeking goodly pearls: 46 Who, when he had found one pearl of great price, went and sold all that he had, and brought it. 47 Again, the **Kingdom of Heaven** is like unto a net, that was cast into the sea, and gathered of every kind: 48 Which, when it was full, they drew to shore, and sat down, and gathered the good into the vessels, but cast the bad away. 49 So shall it be at the end of the world: the angels shall come forth, and sever the wicked from among the just, 50 and shall cast them into the furnace of fire: there shall be wailing and gnashing of teeth. 51 Have ye understood all these things? 52 Therefore every scribe instructed unto the **Kingdom of Heaven**, is like unto a man a householder, which bringeth forth out his treasure new and old.
13:57 A prophet is not without honor, save in his own country, and in his own house.

14:16 They need not depart; give ye them to eat.
14:18 Bring them hither to **ME.**
14:27 Be of good cheer; it is **I**; be not afraid.
14:29 Come.
14:31 O thou of little faith, wherefore didst thou doubt?

15:3 Why do ye also transgress the **COMMAND of GOD** by your traditions? 4 For **GOD Commanded**, saying, Honor thy father and mother: and, He that curseth father or mother, let him die the death. 5

The Blood of Christ

But ye say, Whosoever shall say to father or mother, a gift, by whatsoever thou mightest be profited by me; 6 and honor not his father or his mother. Thus have ye made the **Commandment of GOD** of none effect by your tradition. 7 Hypocrites well did Esaias prophesy of you saying, 8 This people draweth nigh unto **ME** with their mouth, and honoreth **ME** with lips; but their heart is far from **ME**. 9 But in vain they do worship **ME**, teaching doctrines the commandments of men. 10 Hear, and understand: 11 Not that which goeth into the mouth defileth a man: but that which cometh out of the mouth, this defileth a man.

15:13 Every plant, which **MY Heavenly FATHER** hath not planted, shall be rooted up.14 Let them alone: they be blind leaders of the blind. And if the blind lead the blind, both shall fall into the ditch.

15:16 Are ye also yet without understanding? 17 Do not ye yet understand, that whatsoever entereth in at mouth goeth into the belly, and is cast out into the draught? 18 But those things which proceed out of the mouth comes forth from the heart; and they defile the man. 19 For out of the heart proceeds evil thoughts, murders, adulteries, fornications, thefts, false witness, blasphemies: 20 these are which defile a man: but to eat with unwashen hands defileth not a man.

15:24 I AM not sent but unto the lost sheep of the house of Israel.

15:26 It is not meet to take the children's bread, and to cast to dogs.

15:28 O woman, great thy faith: be it unto thee even as thou wilt.

15:32 I have compassion on the multitude, because they continue with **ME** now three days, and have nothing to eat: and **I** will not send them away fasting, lest they faint in the way.

15:34 How many loaves have ye?

16:2 When it is evening, ye say fair weather: for the sky is red. 3 And in the morning, foul weather today: for the sky is red and lowering. O hypocrites, ye can discern the face of the sky; but can ye not the signs of the times? 4 A wicked and adulterous generation seeketh after a sign: and there shall no sign be given unto it, but the sign of the prophet Jonas.

16:6 Take heed and beware of the leaven of the Pharisees and of the Sadducees.

16:8 O ye of little faith, why reason ye among yourselves, because ye have brought no bread? 9 Do ye not understand, neither remember the five loaves of the five thousand, and how many baskets ye took up? 10 neither the seven loaves of the four thousand, and how many baskets ye took up? 11 How is it that ye do not understand that **I** spake not to you concerning bread, that ye should beware of the leaven of the Pharisees and the Sadducees?
16:13 Whom do men say that **I**, the **SON of MAN, AM**?
16:15 But whom say ye that **I AM**?
16:17 Blessed art thou, Simon Bar-jona: for flesh and blood hath not revealed unto thee, but **MY FATHER which is in Heaven**. 18 And **I** say also unto thee, That thou art Peter, and upon this rock **I** will build **MY Church**; and the gates of hell shall not prevail against it. 19 And **I** will give unto thee the keys of the **Kingdom of Heaven**: and whatsoever thou shalt bind on Earth shall be bound in **Heaven**: and whatsoever thou shalt loose on Earth shall be loosed in **Heaven**.
16:23 Get thee behind **ME,** Satan: thou art an offense unto **ME**: for thou savourest not the things that be of **GOD**, but those that be of men. 24 If any will come after **ME**, let him deny himself, and take up his cross, and follow **ME**. 25 For whosoever will save his life shall lose it, and whosoever will lose his life for **MY** sake shall find it. 26 For what is a man profited, if he shall gain the whole world, and lose his own soul? or what shall a man give in exchange for his soul? 27 For the **SON of MAN** shall come in the **Glory** of **HIS FATHER** with **HIS** angels; and then **HE** shall reward every man according to his works. 28 Verily, **I** say unto you, There be some standing here, which shall not taste of death, till they see the **SON of MAN** coming in **HIS Kingdom**.

17:7 Arise, and be not afraid.
17:9 Tell the vision to no man, until the **SON of MAN** be risen again from the dead.
17:11 Elias truly shall first come, and restore all things. 12 But **I** say unto you, That Elias is come already, and they knew him not, but have done unto him whatsoever they listed. Likewise shall also the **SON of MAN** suffer of them.

17:17 O faithless and perverse generation, how long shall **I** be with you? how long shall **I** suffer you? bring him hither to **ME**.

17:20 Because of your unbelief: for verily **I** say unto you, If ye have faith as a grain of mustard seed, ye shall say unto this mountain, Remove hence to yonder place; and it shall remove; and nothing shall be impossible unto you. 21 Howbeit this kind goeth not out but by prayer and fasting. 22 The **SON of MAN** shall be betrayed into the the hands of men: 23 and they shall kill **HIM**, and the third day **HE** shall raised again.

17:25 What thinkest thou, Simon? of whom do the kings of the Earth take custom or tribute? of their own children, or of strangers? 26 Then are the children free. 27 Notwithstanding, lest we should offend them, go to the sea, and cast a hook, and take up the fish that first cometh up; and when thou hast opened his mouth, thou shalt find a piece of money: that take, and give unto them for **ME** and thee.

18:3 Verily, **I** say unto you, Except ye be converted, and become as little children, ye shall not enter into the **Kingdom of Heaven.** 4 Whosoever therefore shall humble himself as this little child, the same is greatest in the **Kingdom of Heaven.** 5 And whoso shall receive one such little child in **MY NAME** receiveth **ME**. 6 But whoso shall offend one of these little ones which believe in **ME**, it were better for him that a millstone were hanged about his neck, and he were drowned in the depth of the sea. 7 Woe until the world because of offences! for it must needs be that offenses come, but woe to that man by whom the offense cometh! 8 Wherefore if thy hand or thy foot offend thee: cut them off, and cast from thee: it is better for thee to enter into life halt or maimed, rather than having two hands or two feet to be cast into everlasting fire. 9 And if thine eye offend thee, pluck it out, and cast from thee: it is better for thee to enter into life with one eye, rather than having two eyes to be cast into hell fire. 10 Take heed that ye despise no not one of these little ones; for **I** say unto you, That in **Heaven** their angels do always behold the face of **MY FATHER which is in Heaven.** 11 For the **SON of MAN** is come to save that which was lost. 12 How think ye? if a man have a hundred sheep, and one of them be gone astray, doth he not leave the ninety and nine, and goeth into the mountains, and seeketh that which is gone astray? 13 And if so be that he find it, verily, **I** say unto you, he rejoiceth more of that than of the ninety and nine which went not astray. 14 Even so it is not the **WILL** of your **FATHER** which is in **Heaven**, that one of these little ones should perish. 15 Moreover if thy brother shall trespass against thee, go and tell him his fault between thee and him alone: if he shall hear thee, thou hast gained thy brother. 16 But if he will not hear, take with thee one or two more, that in the mouth of two or three witnesses every word may be established. 17 And if he shall neglect to hear them, tell unto the church: but if he neglect to hear the church, let him be unto thee as a heathen man and a publican. 18 Verily, **I** say unto you, Whatsoever ye shall bind on Earth shall be bound in **Heaven**; and whatsoever ye shall loose on Earth shall be loosed in Heaven. 19 Again **I** say unto you, That if two of you shall agree on Earth as touching any thing that they shall ask, it shall be done for them of **MY FATHER** which is in **Heaven**. 20 For where two or three are gathered together in **MY NAME**, there am **I** in the midst of them.

18:22 I say not unto thee, Unto seven times: but, Until seventy times seven. 23 Therefore is the **Kingdom of Heaven** likened unto a certain king, which would take account of his servants. 24 And when he had begun to reckon, one was brought unto him, which owed him ten thousand talents. 25 But forasmuch as he had not to pay, his lord commanded him to be sold, and his wife, and children, and all he had, and payment to be made. 26 The servant therefore fell down, and worshipped him, saying, Lord, have patience with me, and I will pay thee all. 27 Then the lord of that servant was moved with compassion, and loosed him, and forgave him the debt. 28 But the same servant went out, and found one of his fellow servants, which owed him a hundred pence: and he laid hands on him, and took him by the throat, saying, Pay me that thou owest. 29 And his fellow servant fell down at his feet, and besought him, saying, Have patience with me, and I will pay thee all. 30 And he would not; but went and cast him into prison, till he should pay the debt. 31 So when his fellow servants saw what was done, they were very sorry, and came and told unto their lord all that was done. 32 Then his lord, after that he had called him, said unto him, O thou wicked servant, I forgave thee all that debt, because thou desirest me:

33 Shouldn't not thou also have had compassion on thy fellow servant, even as I had pity on thee? 34 And his lord was wroth, and delivered him to the tormentors, till he should pay all that was due unto him. 35 So likewise shall **MY Heavenly FATHER** do also unto you, if ye from your hearts forgive not everyone his brother their trespasses.

19:4 Have ye not read, that **HE** which made at the beginning made them male and female, 5 and said, For this cause shall a man leave his father and mother, and shall cleave to his wife: and they twain shall be one flesh? 6 Wherefore they are no more twain, but one flesh. What therefore **GOD** hath joined together, let no man put asunder.

19:8 Moses because of the hardness of your hearts suffered you to put away your wives: but from the beginning it was not so. 9 And **I** say unto you, Whosoever shall put away his wife, except for fornication, and shall marry another committeth adultery: and whosoever marrieth her which is put away doth commit adultery.

19:11 All cannot receive this saying, save to whom it is given. 12 For there are some eunuchs, which were so born from mother's womb: and there are some eunuchs, which were made of men: and there be eunuchs, which have made themselves eunuchs for the **Kingdom of Heaven's** sake. He that is able to receive, let him receive.

19:14 Suffer little children, and forbid them not, to come unto **ME**; for of such is the **Kingdom of Heaven**.

19:17 Why callest thou **ME** good? none good but **ONE, GOD**: but if thou wilt enter into life, keep the commandments. 18 Thou shalt do no murder, Thou shalt not commit adultery, Thou shalt not steal, Thou shalt not bear false witness, 19 Honor thy father and mother: and, Thou shalt love thy neighbor as thyself.

19:21 If thou wilt be perfect, go sell that thou hast, and give to the poor, and thou shalt have treasure in **Heaven**: and come follow **ME**.

19:23 Verily, **I** say unto you, That a rich man shall hardly enter into the **Kingdom of Heaven**. 24 And again **I** say unto you, It is easier for a camel to go through the eye of a needle than for a rich man to enter into the **Kingdom of GOD**.

19:26 With men this is impossible, but with **GOD** all things are possible.

19:28 Verily **I** say unto you, That ye which have followed **ME**, in the regeneration when the **SON of MAN** shall sit on the throne of **HIS GLORY**, ye also shall sit upon twelve thrones, judging the twelve tribes of Israel. 29 And every one that hath forsaken houses, or brethren, or sisters, or father, or mother, or wife, or children, or lands, for **MY NAME's** sake, shall receive a hundredfold, and shall inherit everlasting life. 30 But many first shall be last; and the last first.

20:1 For the **Kingdom of Heaven** is like unto a man a householder, which went out early in the morning to hire laborers into his vineyard. 2 And when he agreed with the laborers for a penny a day, he sent them into his vineyard. 3 And he went out about the third hour, and saw others standing idle in the market place, 4 And say unto them; Go ye also into the vineyard, and whatsoever is right I will give you. And they went their way. 5 Again he went out about the sixth and ninth hour, and did likewise. 6 And about the eleventh hour he went out, and found others standing idle, and saith unto them, Why stand ye here all the day idle? 7 They say unto him, Because no man hath hired us. He saith unto them, Go ye also into the vineyard; and whatsoever is right, shall ye receive. 8 So when even was come, the lord of the vineyard saith unto his steward, Call the laborers, and give them hire, beginning from the last unto the first. 9 And when they came that about the eleventh hour, they received every man a penny. 10 But when the first came, they supposed that they should have received more; and they likewise received every man a penny. 11 And when they had received, they murmured against the goodman of the house, 12 Saying, These last have wrought one hour, and thou hast made them equal unto us, which have borne the burden and heat of the day. 13 But he answered one of them, and said, Friend, I do thee no wrong: didst not thou agree with me for a penny? 14 Take thine, and go thy way: I will give unto this last, even as unto thee. 15 Is it not lawful for me to do what I will with mine own? Is thine eye evil, because I am good? 16 So the last shall be first, and the first last; for many be called, but few chosen.

20:18 Behold, we go up to Jerusalem; and the **SON of MAN** shall be betrayed unto the chief priests and unto his scribes, and they shall condemn **HIM** to death, 19 And shall deliver **HIM** to the Gentiles to mock, and to scrounge, and to crucify, and the third day **HE** shall rise again.

20:21 What wilt thou? 22 Ye know not what ye ask. Are ye able to drink of the cup that **I** shall drink of, and to be baptized with the baptism that **I AM** baptized with? 23 Ye shall drink indeed the cup, and be baptized with the baptism that **I AM** baptized with: but to sit on **MY** right hand, and on **MY** left, is not **MINE** to give, but for whom it is prepared of **MY FATHER**. **20:25** Ye know that the princes of the Gentiles exercise dominion over them, and they that are great exercise authority upon them. 26 But it shall not be so among you: but whosoever will be great among you, let him be your minister; 27 And whosoever will be chief among you, let him be your servant: 28 Even as the **SON of MAN** came not to be ministered unto, but to minister, and to give **HIS** life a ransom for many.

20:32 What will ye that **I** shall do unto you?

21:2 Go unto the village over against you, and straightway ye shall find an ass tied, and a colt with her: loose, and bring unto **ME**. 3 And if any say aught unto you, ye shall say, The **LORD** hath need of them: and straightway he will send them.

21:13 It is written, **MY House** shall be called the **House of Prayers**; but ye have made it a den of thieves.

21:16 Yea; have ye never read, Out of the mouth of babes and sucklings **THOU** hast perfected praise?

21:19 Let no fruit grow on thee henceforward for ever.

21:21 Verily **I** say unto you, If ye have faith, and doubt not, ye shall not only do this to the fig tree, but also if ye shall say unto this mountain, Be thou removed, and be thou cast into the sea; it shall be done. 22 And all things, whatever ye shall ask in prayer, believing, ye shall receive.

21:24 **I** also will ask you one thing, which if ye tell **ME**, **I** in like wise will tell you by what authority **I** do these things. 25 The baptism of John, whence was it? from **Heaven**, or men? **21:27** Neither tell **I** you

by what authority **I** do these things. 28 But what think ye? A man had two sons: and he came to the first, and said, Son, go work today in my vineyard. 29 He answered and said, I will not; but afterward he repented, and went. 30 And he came to the second, and said likewise. And he answered and said, I go, sir; and went not. 31 Whether of the twain did the will of the father? Verily **I** say unto you, That publicans and the harlots go into the **Kingdom of GOD** before you. 32 For John came unto you in the way of righteousness, and ye believed him not; but the publicans and the harlots believed him: and ye, when ye had seen, repented not afterward, that ye might believe him. 33 Hear another parable: There was a certain householder, which planted a vineyard, and hedged it round about, and digged a winepress in it, and built a tower, and let it out to husbandmen, and went into a far country: 34 And when the time of the fruit drew near, he sent his servants to the husbandmen, that they might receive the fruit of it. 35 And the husbandmen took his servants, and beat one, and killed another, and stoned another. 36 Again, he sent other servants more than the first: and they did unto them likewise. 37 But last of all he sent unto them his son, saying, They will reverence my son. 38 But when the husbandmen saw the son, they said among themselves, This is the heir; come let us kill him, and let us seize on his inheritance. 39 And they caught him, and cast out of the vineyard, and slew. 40 When the lord therefore of the vineyard cometh, what will he do unto those husbandmen?
21:42 Did ye never read in the scriptures, The **STONE** which the builders rejected, the **SAME** is become the **HEAD of the corner**: this is the **LORD's** doing, and it is marvelous in our eyes? 43 Therefore say **I** unto you, the **Kingdom of GOD** shall be taken from you, and given to a nation bringing forth the fruits thereof. 44 And whosoever shall fall on this **STONE** shall be broken: but on whomsoever **IT** shall fall, **IT** will grind him to powder.

22:2 The **Kingdom of Heaven** is like unto a certain king, which made a marriage for his son, 3 And sent forth his servants to call them that were bidden to the wedding: and they would not come. 4 Again, he sent forth other servants, saying, Tell them which are bidden, Behold, I have

THE BLOOD OF CHRIST

prepared my dinner: my oxen and fatlings killed, and all things ready: come unto the marriage. 5 But they made light of, and went their ways, one to his farm, another to his merchandise: 6 And the remnant took his servants, and entreated spitefully, and slew. 7 But when the king heard, he was wroth: and he sent forth his armies, and destroyed those murderers, and burned up their city. 8 Then saith he to his servants, The wedding is ready, but they which were bidden were not worthy. 9 Go ye therefore into the highways, and as many as ye find, bid to the marriage. 10 So those servants went into the highways, and gathered together all as many as they found, both bad and good: and the wedding was furnished with guests. 11 And when the king came in to see the guests, he saw there a man which had not on a wedding garment: 12 And he saith unto him, Friend, how camest thou in hither not having a wedding garment? And he was speechless. 13 Then said the king to the servants, Bind him hand and foot, and take him away, and cast out into outer darkness; there shall be weeping and gnashing of teeth. 14 For many are called, but few chosen. **22:18** Why tempt **ME**, hypocrites? 19 Show **ME** the tribute money. 20 Whose this image and superscription? 21 Render therefore Caesar the things which are Caesar's; and unto **GOD** the things of **GOD's**.
22:29 Ye do err, not knowing the Scriptures, nor the power of **GOD**. 30 For in the resurrection they neither marry, nor are given in marriage, but are as the angels of **GOD in Heaven**. 31 But as touching the resurrection of the dead, have ye not read that which was spoken unto you by **GOD**, saying, 32 **I AM** the **GOD** of Abraham, and the **GOD** of Isaac, and the **GOD** of Jacob? **GOD** is not the **GOD** of the dead, but of the living.
22:37 Thou shalt love the **LORD** thy **GOD** with all thy heart, and with all thy soul, and with all thy mind. 38 This is the first and great **Commandment**. 39 And the second like unto it, Thou shalt love thy neighbor as thyself. 40 On these two **Commandments** hang all the law and prophets.
22:42 What think ye of **CHRIST**? whose **SON** is **HE**? 43 How then doth David in spirit call **HIM LORD**, saying, 44 The **LORD** saith unto my **LORD**, Sit **THOU** on **MY** right hand, till **I** make **THINE** enemies **THY** footstool? 45 If David then call **HIM LORD**, how **HE** his son?

23:2 The Scribes and the Pharisees sit in Moses' seat: 3 All therefore whatsoever they bid you observe, observe and do; but do not ye after their works: for they say, and do not. 4 For they bind heavy burdens and grievous to be borne, and lay on men's shoulders; but they will not move them with one of their fingers. 5 But all their works they do for to be seen of men: they make broad their phylacteries, and enlarge the borders of their garments, 6 And love the uppermost rooms at feasts, and the chief seats in the synagogues, 7 And greetings in the markets, and to be called of men Rabbi, Rabbi. 8 But be not ye called Rabbi: for **ONE** is your **MASTER, CHRIST**; and all ye are brethren. 9 And call no your father upon the Earth: for **ONE** is your **FATHER**, which is in **Heaven**. 10 Neither be ye called masters: for **ONE** is your **MASTER, CHRIST.** 11 But he that is greatest among you shall be your servant. 12 And whosoever shall exalt himself shall be abased; and he that shall humble himself shall be exalted. 13 But woe unto you, scribes and Pharisees, hypocrites! for ye shut up the **Kingdom of Heaven** against men: for ye neither go in,neither suffer ye them that entering to go in. 14 Woe unto you scribes and Pharisees, hypocrites! for ye devour widow's houses, and for a pretense make long prayer: therefore ye shall receive the greater damnation. Woe unto you, scribes and Pharisees, hypocrites! for ye compass sea and land to make one proselyte, and when he is made, ye make him twofold more the child of hell than yourselves. 16 Woe unto you, blind guides, which say, Whosoever shall swear by the temple, it is nothing; but whosoever shall swear by the gold of the temple, he is a debtor! 17 Fools and blind: for whether greater, the gold or the temple that sanctifieth the gold? 18 And, Whosoever shall swear by the altar, it is nothing: but whosoever sweareth by the gift that is upon it, he is guilty. 19 Fools and blind: for whether greater, the gift, or the altar that sanctifieth the gift? 20 Whoso therefore shall swear by the altar, sweareth by it, and by all things thereon. 21 And whoso shall swear by the temple, sweareth by it, and by **HIM** that dwelleth therein. 22 And he that shall swear by **Heaven**, sweareth by the throne of **GOD**, and by **HIM** that sitteth thereon. 23 Woe unto you,scribes and Pharisees, hypocrites! for ye pay tithe of mint and anise and cummin, and have omitted the weightier of the law, judgment, mercy, and faith: these ought ye to have done,

The Blood of Christ

and not to leave the other undone. 24 Blind guides, which strain a gnat, and swallow a camel. 25 Woe unto you, scribes and Pharisees, hypocrites! for ye make clean the outside of the cup and of the platter, but within they are full of extortion and excess. 26 Blind Pharisees, cleanse first that within the cup and platter, that the outside of them may be clean also. 27 Woe unto you, scribes and Pharisees, hypocrites! for ye are like unto whited sepulchres, which indeed appear beautiful outward, but are within full of dead bones, and of all uncleanness. 28 Even so ye also outwardly appear righteous unto men, but within ye are full of hypocrisy and iniquity. 29 Woe unto you scribes and Pharisees, hypocrites! because ye built the tombs of the prophets, and garnish the sepulchres of the righteous, 30 And say, If we had been in the days of our fathers, we would not have been partakers with them in the blood of the prophets. 31 Wherefore ye be witnesses unto yourselves, that ye are the children of them which killed the prophets. 32 Fill ye up then the measure of your fathers. 33 Serpents, generation of vipers, how can ye escape the damnation of hell? 34 Wherefore, behold, **I** send unto you prophets, and wise men, and scribes: and of them ye shall kill and crucify; and of them shall ye scourge in your synagogues, and persecute from city to city: 35 That upon you may come all the righteous blood shed upon the Earth, from the blood of righteous Abel unto the blood of Zacharias son of Barachias, whom ye slew between the temple and the altar. 36 Verily **I** say unto you, All these things shall come upon this generation. 37 O Jerusalem, Jerusalem, that killest the prophets, and stonest them which are sent unto thee, how often would I have gathered thy children together, even as a hen gathereth her chickens under wings, and ye would not! 38 Behold, your house is left unto you desolate. 39 For **I** say unto you, Ye shall not see **ME** henceforth, till ye shall say, Blessed **HE** that cometh in the **NAME of the LORD**.

24:2 See ye not all these things? verily **I** say unto you, There shall not be left here one stone upon another, that shall be thrown down. **24:4** Take heed that no man deceive you. 5 For many shall come in **MY NAME**, saying, I am **CHRIST;** and shall deceive many. 6 And ye shall hear of wars and rumors of wars: see that ye be not troubled: for all must come to pass, but the end is not yet. 7 For nation shall rise against nation, and kingdom against kingdom: and there shall be famines, and pestilences, and earthquakes, in divers places. 8 All these the beginning of sorrows. 9 Then shall they deliver you up to be afflicted, and kill you: and ye shall be hated of all nations for **MY NAME's** sake. 10 And then shall many be offended, and shall betray one another, and shall hate one another. 11 And many false prophets shall arise, and shall deceive many. 12 And because iniquity shall abound, the love of many shall wax cold. 13 But he that shall endure unto the end, the same shall be saved. 14 And this **GOSPEL of the Kingdom** shall be preached in all the world for a witness unto all nations; and then shall the end come. 15 When ye therefore shall see the abomination of desolation, spoken of by Daniel the prophet, stand in the Holy Place, (whoso readeth, let him understand,) 16 Then let them which be in Judaea flee into the mountains: 17 Let him which is on the housetop not come down to take anything out of his house: 18 Neither let him which is in the field return back to take his clothes. 19 And woe unto them that are with child, and to them that give suck in those days! 20 But pray ye that your flight be not in winter, neither on the sabbath day: 21 For then shall be great tribulation, such as was not since the beginning of the world to this time, no, nor ever shall be. 22 And except those days should be shortened, there shall no flesh be saved: but for the elect's sake those days shall be shortened. 23 Then if any man shall say unto you, Lo here **CHRIST**, or there: believe not. 24 For there shall arise false christs, and false prophets, and shall show great signs and wonders; insomuch that, if possible, they shall deceive the very elect. 25 Behold, **I** have told you before, 26 Wherefore if they shall say unto you, Behold, **HE** is in the desert; go not forth: behold, in the secret chambers; believe not. 27 For as the lightning cometh out of the east, and shineth even unto the west; so shall also the coming of the **SON of MAN** be. 28 For wheresoever the carcass is, there will be the eagles gathered together. 29 Immediately after the tribulation of those days shall the sun be darkened, and the moon shall not give her light, and the stars shall fall from **Heaven**, and the powers of the **Heavens** shall be shaken: 30 And then shall appear the sign of the **SON of MAN** in **Heaven**: and then shall all the tribes of the Earth mourn, and they shall see the **SON of MAN** coming in the clouds of **Heaven** with **Power** and great **Glory**. 31 And **HE** shall send **HIS** angels with a great sound of a trumpet, and they shall gather together **HIS** elect from the four winds, from one end of **Heaven** to the **other**. 32 Now learn a parable of the fig tree; When the branch is yet tender, and putteth forth leaves, ye know that summer is nigh: 33 So likewise ye, when ye shall see all these things, know that it is near, at the doors. 34 Verily **I** say unto you, This generation shall not pass, till all these things be fulfilled. 35 **Heaven** and **Earth** shall pass away, but **MY WORDS** shall not pass away. 36 But of that day and hour knoweth no, no, not the angels of **Heaven**, but **MY FATHER** only. 37 But as the days of Noe, so shall also the coming of the **SON of MAN** be. 38 For as in the days that were before the flood they were eating and drinking, marrying and giving in marriage, until the day Noe entered into the ark, 39 And knew not until the flood came, and took them all away; so shall also the **SON of MAN** be. 40 Then shall two be in the field; the one shall be taken, and the other left. 41 Two grinding at the mill; the one shall be taken, and the other left. 42 Watch therefore; for ye know not what hour your **LORD** doth come. 43 But know this, that if the goodman of the house had known in what watch the thief would come, he would have watched, and would not have suffered his house to be broken up. 44 Therefore be ye also ready: for in such an hour as ye think not the **SON of MAN** cometh. 45 Who then is a faithful and wise servant, whom his **LORD** hath made ruler over **HIS Household**, to give them meat in due season? 46 Blessed that servant, whom his **LORD** when **HE** cometh shall find so doing. 47 Verily **I** say unto you, That **HE** shall make him ruler over all **HIS Goods**. 48 But and if that evil servant shall say in his heart, my **LORD** delayeth **HIS** coming; 49 And shall begin to smite fellow servants, and to eat and drink with the drunken; 50 The **LORD** of that servant shall come in a day when he looketh not for, and in a hour that he is not aware of, 51 And shall cut him asunder, and appoint his portion with the hypocrites: there shall be weeping and gnashing of teeth.

25:1 Then shall the **Kingdom of Heaven** be likened unto ten virgins, which took their lamps, and went forth to meet the bridegroom. 2

And five of them were wise, and five foolish. 3 They that foolish took their lamps, and took no oil with them: 4 But the wise took oil in their vessels with their lamps. 5 While the bridegroom tarried, they all slumbered and slept. 6 And at midnight there was a cry made, Behold, the bridegroom cometh; go ye out to meet him. 7 Then all the virgins arose, and trimmed their lamps. 8 And the foolish said unto the wise, Give us of your oil; for our lamps are gone out. 9 But the wise answered, saying, lest there be not enough for us and you: but go ye rather to them that sell, and buy for yourselves. 10 And while they went to buy, the bridegroom came; and they which were ready went in with him to the marriage: and the door was shut. 11 Afterward came also the other virgins, saying, **LORD, LORD,** open to us. 12 But **HE** answered and said, Verily **I** say unto you, **I** know you not. 13 Watch therefore; for ye know neither the day nor the hour wherein the **SON of MAN** cometh. 14 For as a man traveling into a far country, called his own servants, and delivered unto them his goods. 15 And unto one he gave five talents, to another two, and to another one; to every man according to his several ability; and straightway took his journey. 16 Then he that received five talents went and traded with the same, and made other five talents. 17 And likewise he that two, he also gained other two. 18 But he that had received one went and digged in the earth, and hid his lord's money. 19 After a long time the lord of those servants cometh, and reckoneth with them. 20 And so he that had received five talents came and brought other five talents, saying, Lord, thou deliverest unto me five talents: behold, I have gained beside them five talents more. 21 His lord said unto him, Well done, good and faithful servant: thou hast been faithful over a few things, I will make thee ruler over many things; enter thou into the joy of thy lord. 22 He also that received two talents came and said, Lord, thou deliverest unto me two talents: behold, I have gained two other talents beside them. 23 His lord said unto him, Well done, good and faithful servant; thou hast been faithful over a few things. I will make thee ruler over many things: enter thou into the joy of thy lord. 24 Then he which had received the one talent came and said, Lord, I knew that thou art a hard man, reaping where thou hast not sown, and gathering where thou hast not strewed: 25 And I was afraid, and went and hid thy talent in the earth: lo, thou hast thine. 26 His lord answered and said unto him, wicked and slothful servant, thou knewest that I reap where I sowed not, and gather where I have not strewed; 27 Thou oughtest therefore to have put my money to the exchangers, and at my coming I should have received mine own with usury. 28 Take therefore the talent from him, and give to him which hath the ten talents. 29 For unto every one that hath shall be given, and he shall have abundance: but from him that hath not shall be taken away even that which he hath. 30 And cast ye the unprofitable servant into outer darkness: there shall be weeping and gnashing of teeth. 31 When the **SON of MAN** shall come in **HIS GLORY**, and all the holy angels with **HIM**, then shall **He** sit upon the throne of **HIS GLORY**: 32 And before **HIM** shall be gathered all nations: and **HE** shall separate them one from another, as a shepherd divideth sheep from goats: 33 And **HE** shall set the sheep on **HIS** right hand, but the goats on the left. 34 Then shall the **KING** say unto them on **HIS** right hand, Come, ye blessed of **MY FATHER**, inherit the **Kingdom** prepared for you from the foundation of the world: 35 For **I** was ahungered, and ye gave **ME** meat: **I** was thirsty, and you gave **ME** drink: **I** was a stranger, and ye took **ME** in: 36 Naked, and ye clothed **ME**: **I** was sick, and ye visited **ME**: **I** was in prison, and ye came unto **ME**. 37 Then shall the righteous answer **HIM**, saying, **LORD**, when saw **THEE** ahungered, and fed? or thirsty, and gave drink? 38 When saw we **THEE** a stranger, and took in? or naked, and clothed? 39 Or when saw we **THEE** sick, or in prison, and came unto **THEE**? 40 And the **KING** shall answer and say unto them. Verily **I** say unto you, Inasmuch as ye have done unto one of the least of these **MY** brethren, ye have done unto **ME**. 41 Then shall **HE** say also unto them on the left hand, Depart from **ME,** ye cursed, into everlasting fire, prepared for the devil and his angels: 42 For **I** was ahungered, and ye gave **ME** no meat: **I** was thirsty, and ye gave **ME** no drink: 43 **I** was a stranger, and ye took **ME** not in: naked, and ye clothed **ME** not: sick, and in prison, and ye visited **ME** not. 44 Then shall they answer **HIM**, saying, **LORD**, when saw we **THEE** ahungered, or athirst, or a stranger, or naked, or sick, or in prison, and did not ministered unto **THEE**? 45 Then shall **HE** answer them, saying, Verily **I** say unto you, Inasmuch as ye did not to one of the least of these, ye did not to **ME**. 46 And these shall go away into everlasting punishment: but the righteous into life eternal.

26:2 Ye know that after two days is the Passover, and the **SON of MAN** is betrayed to be crucified.

26:10 Why trouble ye the woman? for she hath wrought a good work upon **ME**. 11 For ye have the poor always with you; but **ME** ye have not always. 12 For in that she hath poured this ointment on **MY** body, she did for **MY** burial. 13 Verily **I** say unto you, Wheresoever this gospel shall be preached in the world, shall also this, that this woman hath done, be told for a memorial for her.

26:18 Go into the city to such a man, and say unto him, The **MASTER** saith, **MY** time is at hand; **I** will keep the Passover at thy house with **MY** disciples.

26:21 Verily **I** say unto you, that one of you shall betray **ME**.

26:23 He that dipped hand with **ME** in the dish, the same shall betray **ME**. 24 The **SON of MAN** goeth as it is written of **HIM**: but woe unto that man by whom the **SON of MAN** is betrayed! it had been good for that man if he had not been born. 25 Thou hast said. 26 Take, eat; this **MY** body. 27 Drink ye all of it; 28 For this is **MY** blood of the new testament, which is shed for many for the remission of sins. 29 But **I** say unto you, **I** will not drink henceforth of this fruit of the vine, until that day when **I** drink it new with you in **MY FATHER's** Kingdom.

26:31 All ye shall be offended because of **ME** this night: for it is written, **I** will smite the shepherd, and the sheep of the flock shall be scattered abroad. 32 But after **I AM** risen again, **I** will go before you in Galilee.

26:34 Verily **I** say unto thee, That this night, before the cock crow, thou shalt deny **ME** thrice.

26:36 Sit ye here, while **I** go and pray yonder.

26:38 MY soul is exceeding sorrowful, even unto death: tarry ye here, and watch with **ME**. 39 O **MY FATHER**, if it be possible, let this cup pass from **ME**: nevertheless, not as **I** will, but as **THOU**. 40 What, could you not watch with **ME** one hour! 41 Watch and pray, that ye enter not into temptation: the spirit indeed willing, but the flesh weak. 42 O **MY FATHER**, if this cup may not pass away from **ME**, except **I** drink it, **THY** will be done.

26:45 Sleep on now, and take rest: behold, the hour is at hand, and the **SON of MAN** is betrayed into the hands of sinners. 46 Rise, let us be going: behold, he is at hand that doth betray **ME**.

26:50 Friend, wherefore art thou come?
26:52 Put up thy sword into his place: for all they that take the sword shall perish with the sword. 53 Thinkest thou that **I** cannot pray to **MY FATHER**, and **HE** shall presently give **ME** more than twelve legions of angels? 54 But how then shall the Scriptures be fulfilled, that thus it must be? 55 Are ye come out as against a thief with swords and staves for to take **ME**? **I** sat daily with you teaching in the temple, and ye laid no hold on **ME**. 56 But all this was done, that the Scriptures of the prophets might be fulfilled.
26:64 Thou hast said: nevertheless **I** say unto you, Hereafter, shall ye see the **SON of MAN** sitting on the right hand of power, and coming in the clouds of Heaven.
26:75 Before the cock crow, thou shalt deny **ME** thrice.

27:11 Thou sayest.
27:46 Eli, Eli, lamasabach' thani? **MY GOD, MY GOD**, why hast **THOU** forsaken **ME**.
27:63 After three days **I** will rise again.

28:9 All hail. 10 Be not afraid: go tell **MY** brethren that they go into Galilee, and there shall they see **ME**.
28:18 All **POWER** is given unto **ME** in **Heaven** and in **Earth**. 19 Go ye therefore, and teach all nations, baptizing them in the **NAME of the FATHER, and of the SON, and of the HOLY GHOST**; 20 Teaching them to observe all things whatsoever **I** have commanded you: and, lo, **I AM** with you alway, unto the end of the world. **AMEN**

What JESUS Said
MARK

1:15 The time is fulfilled, and the **Kingdom of GOD** is at hand: repent ye, and believe the gospel.
1:17 Come ye after **ME**, and **I** will make you to become fishers of men.
1:25 Hold thy peace, and come out of him.
1:38 Let us go into the next towns, that **I** may preach there also: for therefore came **I** forth.
1:41 **I** will; be thou clean.
1:44 See thou say nothing to any man: but go thy way, show thyself to the priest, and offer for thy cleansing those things which Moses commanded, for a testimony unto them.

2:5 Son, thy sins be forgiven thee.
2:8 Why reason ye these things in your heart? 9 Whether is it easier to say to the sick of the palsy, sins be forgiven thee; or to say, Arise, and take up thy bed, and walk? 10 But that ye may know that the **SON of MAN** hath power on Earth to forgive sins, 11 **I** say unto thee, Arise, and take up thy bed, and go thy way into thine house.
2:14 Follow **ME**.
2:17 They that are whole have no need of the physician, but they that are sick: **I** came not to call the righteous, but sinners to repentance.
2:19 Can the children of the bridechamber fast, while the bridegroom is with them? As long as they have the bridegroom with them, they cannot fast. 20 But the days will come, when the bridegroom shall be taken away from them, and then shall they fast in those days. 21 No man also seweth a piece of new cloth on an old garment; else the new piece that filled it up taketh away from the old, and the rent is made worse. 22 And no man putteth new wine into old bottles; else the new wine doth burst the bottles, and the wine is spilled, and the bottles will be marred: but new wine must be put into new bottles.
2:25 Have ye never read what David did, when he had need, and was ahungered, he, and they that were with him? 26 How he went into the house of **GOD** in the days of Abiathar the high priest, and did eat the showbread, which is not lawful to eat but for the priest, and gave also to them which were with him? 27 The sabbath was made for man, and not man for the sabbath: 28 Therefore the **SON of MAN** is **LORD** also of the sabbath.

3:3 Stand forth. 4 Is it lawful to do good on the sabbath days, or to do evil? To save life, or to kill? 5 Stretch forth thine hand.

3:23 How can Satan cast out Satan? 24 And if a kingdom be divided against itself, that kingdom cannot stand. 25 And if a house be divided against itself, that house cannot stand. 26 And if Satan rise up against himself, and be divided, he cannot stand, but hath an end. 27 No man can enter into a strong man's house, and spoil his goods, except he will first bind the strong man; and then he will spoil his house. 28 Verily I say unto you, All sins shall be forgiven unto the sons of men, and blasphemies wherewith soever they shall blaspheme: 29 But he that shall blaspheme against the **HOLY GHOST** hath never forgiveness, but is in danger of eternal damnation:

3:33 Who is **MY** mother, or **MY** brethren? 34 Behold **MY** mother and **MY** brethren! 35 For whosoever shall do the will of **GOD**, the same is **MY** brother, and **MY** sister, and mother.

4:3 Hearken; Behold, there went out a sower to sow: 4 And it came to pass, as he sowed, some fell by the wayside, and the fowls of the air came and devoured it up. 5 And some fell on stony ground, where it had not much earth; and immediately it sprang up, because it had no depth of earth: 6 But when the sun was up, it was scorched; and because it had no root, it withered away. 7 And some fell among thorns, and the thorns grew up, and choked it, and it yielded no fruit. 8 And other fell on good ground, and did yield fruit that sprang up and increased, and brought forth, some thirty, and some sixty, and some a hundred. 9 He that hath ears to hear, let them hear.

4:11 Unto you it is given to know the mystery of the **Kingdom of GOD**: but unto them that are without, all things are done in parables: 12 That seeing they may see, and not perceive; and hearing they may hear, and not understand; lest at any time they should be converted, and sins should be forgiven them. 13 Know ye not this parable? And how then will ye know all parables? 14 The sower soweth the word. 15 And these are they by the wayside, where the word is sown; but when they have heard, Satan cometh immediately, and taketh away the word that was sown in their hearts. 16 And these are likewise which are sown on stony ground; who, when they have heard the word, immediately receive it with gladness; 17 And have no root in themselves, and so endure but for a time: afterward, when affliction or persecution ariseth for the word's sake, immediately they are offended. 18 And these are they which are sown among thorns; such as hear the word, 19 And the cares of this world, and the deceitfulness of riches, and the lusts of other things entering in, choke the word, and it becometh unfruitful. 20 And these are they which are sown on good ground; such as hear the word, and receive, and bring forth fruit, some thirtyfold, some sixty, and some a hundred. 21 Is a candle brought to be put under a bushel, or under a bed? And not to be set on a candlestick? 22 For there is nothing hid, which shall not be manifested; neither was any thing kept secret, but that it should come abroad. 23 If any man have ears to hear, let him hear. 24 Take heed what ye hear. With what measure ye mete, it shall be measured to you; and unto you that hear shall more be given. 25 For he that hath, to him shall be given; and he that hath not, from him shall be taken even that which he hath. 26 So is the **Kingdom of GOD,** as if a man should cast seed into the ground; 27 And should sleep, and rise night and day, and the seed should spring and grow up, he knoweth not how. 28 For the earth bringeth forth fruit of herself; first the blade, then the ear, after that the full corn in the ear. 29 But when the fruit is brought forth, immediately he putteth in the sickle, because the harvest is come. 30 Whereunto shall we liken the **Kingdom of GOD?** Or with what comparison shall we compare it? 31 Like a grain of mustard seed, which, when it is sown in the earth, is less than all the seeds that be in the earth: 32 But when it is sown, it groweth up, and becometh greater than all herbs, and shooteth out great branches; so that the fowls of the air may lodge under the shadow of it.

4:35 Let us pass over unto the other side.

4:39 Peace, be still. 40 Why are ye so fearful? How is it that ye have no faith?

5:8 Come out of the man, unclean spirit. 9 What thy name?

5:19 Go home to thy friends, and tell them how great things the **LORD** hath done for thee, and hath compassion on thee.

5:30 Who touched **MY** clothes? 31 Who touched **ME**?
5:34 Daughter, thy faith hath made thee whole; go in peace, and be whole of thy plague.
5:36 Be not afraid, only believe.
5:39 Why make ye this ado, and weep? the damsel is not dead, but sleepeth.
5:41 Talitha cumi; Damsel, Arise.

6:4 A prophet is not without honor, but in his own country, and among his own kin, and in his own house.
6:10 In what place soever ye enter into a house, there you abide till ye depart from that place. 11 And whosoever shall not receive you nor hear you, when ye depart thence, shake off the dust under your feet for a testimony against them. Verily **I** say unto you, It shall be more tolerable for Sodom and Gomorrah in the day of judgment, than for that city.
6:31 Come ye yourselves apart into a desert place, and rest a while:
6:37 Give ye them to eat. 38 How many loaves have ye? go and see.
6:50 Be of good cheer; it is **I**; be not afraid.

7:6 Well hath Esaias prophesied of you hypocrites, as it is written, This people honoreth **ME** with lips, but their heart is far from **ME**. 7 Howbeit in vain do they worship **ME**, teaching doctrines the commandments of men. 8 For laying aside the **Commandment of GOD**, ye hold the tradition of men, the washing of pots and cups: and many other such like things ye do. 9 Full well ye reject the **Commandment of GOD**, that ye may keep your own tradition. 10 For Moses said, Honor thy father and thy mother, and, Whoso curseth father or mother, let him die the death: 11 But ye say, If a man shall say to his father or mother, Corban, that is to say, a gift, by whatsoever thou mightest be profited by me; 12 And ye suffer him no more to do aught for his father or his mother; 13 Making the **WORD of GOD** of none effect through your tradition, which ye have delivered: And many such like things do ye. 14 Hearken unto **ME** every one, and understand: 15 There is nothing from without a man, that entering into him can defile him: but the things which come out of him, those are the things that defile the man. 16 If any man have ears to hear, let him hear.

7:18 Are you so without understanding also? Do ye not perceive, that whatsoever thing from without entereth into the man, cannot defile him; 19 Because it entereth not into his heart, but into the belly, and goeth out into the draught, purging all meats? 20 That which cometh out of the man, that defileth the man. 21 For from within, out of the heart of men, proceed evil thoughts, adulteries, fornications, murders, 22 Thefts, covetousness, wickedness, deceit, lasciviousness, an evil eye, blasphemy, pride, foolishness: 23 All these evil things come from within, and defile the man.

7:27 Let the children first be filled: for it is not meet to take the children's bread, and to cast unto the dogs.

7:29 For this saying go thy way; the devil gone out of thy daughter.

7:34 Ephphatha, Be opened.

8:2 I have compassion on the multitude, because they have now been with **ME** three days, and have nothing to eat: 3 And if **I** send them away fasting to their own houses, they will faint by the way: for divers of them came from far.

8:5 How many loaves have ye?

8:12 Why do this generation seek after a sign? verily **I** say unto you, There shall no sign be given unto this generation.

8:15 Take heed, beware of the leaven of the Pharisees, and the leaven of Herod.

8:17 Why reason ye, because ye have no bread? perceive ye not yet, neither understand? have ye yet your heart hardened? 18 Having eyes, see ye not? and having ears, hear ye not? and do ye not remember? 19 When **I** brake the five loaves among the five thousand, how many baskets full of fragments took ye up? 20 And when the seven among four thousand, how many baskets full of fragments took ye up? 21 How is it that ye do not understand?

8:26 Neither go into the town, nor tell to any in the town. 27 Whom do men say that **I AM**?

8:29 But whom say ye that **I AM**?

8:33 Get thee behind **ME**, Satan: for thou savorest not the things that be of **GOD**, but the things that be of men. 34 Whosoever will come after **ME**, let him deny himself, and take up his cross, and follow **ME**. 35 For whosoever will save his life shall lose it; but whosoever shall lose his life for **MY** sake and the **GOSPEL's**, the same shall save it. 36 For what shall it profit a man, if he gain the whole world, and lose his soul? 37 Or what shall a man give in exchange for his soul? 38 Whosoever therefore shall be ashamed of **ME** and of **MY WORDS**, in this adulterous and sinful generation, of him also shall the **SON of MAN** be ashamed, when **HE** cometh in the **GLORY** of **HIS FATHER** with the holy angels.

9:1 Verily **I** say unto you, That there be some of them that stand here, which shall not taste of death, till they have seen the **Kingdom of GOD** come with **Power**.
9:12 Elias verily cometh first, and restoreth all things: and how it is written of the **SON of MAN**, that **HE** must suffer many things, and be set at nought. 13 But **I** say unto you, That Elias is indeed come, and they have done unto him whatsoever they listed, as it is written of him.
9:16 What question ye with them?
9:19 O faithless generation, how long shall **I** be with you? how long shall **I** suffer you? bring him unto **ME**.
9:21 How long is it ago since this came unto him?
9:23 If thou canst believe, all things possible to him that believeth.
9:25 Dumb and deaf spirit, **I** charge thee, come out of him, and enter no more into him.
9:29 This kind can come forth by nothing, but by prayer and fasting.
9:31 The **SON of MAN** is delivered into the hands of men, and they shall kill **HIM**; and after that **HE** is killed, **HE** shall rise the third day.
9:33 What was it that ye disputed among yourselves by the way?
9:35 If any man desire to to be first, shall be last of all, and servant of all.
9:37 Whosoever shall receive one of such children in **MY NAME**, receiveth **ME**; and whosoever receive **ME**, receiveth not **ME**, but **HIM** that sent **ME**.

9:39 Forbid him not: for there is no man which shall do a miracle in **MY NAME**, that can lightly speak evil of **ME**. 40 For he that is not against us is on our part. 41 For whosoever shall give you a cup of water to drink in **MY NAME**, because you belong to **CHRIST**, verily **I** say unto you, he shall not lose his reward. 42 And whosoever shall offend one of little ones that believe in **ME**, it is better for him that a millstone were hanged about his neck, and he were cast into the sea. 43 And if thy hand offend thee, cut it off: it is better for thee to enter into life maimed, than having two hands to go into hell, into the fire that never shall be quenched: 44 Where their worm dieth not, and the fire is not quenched. 45 And if thy foot offend thee, cut it off: it is better for thee to enter halt into life, than having two feet to be cast into hell, into the fire that never shall be quenched. 46 Where their worm dieth not, and the fire is not quenched. 47 And if thine eye offend thee, pluck it out: it is better for thee to enter into the **Kingdom of GOD** with one eye, than having two eyes to be cast into hell fire: 48 Where their worm dieth not, and the fire is not quenched. 49 For every one shall be salted with fire, and every sacrifice shall be salted with salt. 50 Salt good: but if the salt have lost his saltness, wherewith will ye season it? Have salt in yourselves, and have peace one with another.

10:3 What did Moses command you?
10:5 For the hardness of your heart he wrote this precept. 6 But from the beginning of the creation **GOD** made them male and female. 7 For this cause a man leave his father and mother, and cleave to his wife; 8 And they twain shall be one flesh: so then they are no more twain, but one flesh. 9 What therefore **GOD** hath joined together, let no man put asunder.
10:11 Whosoever shall put away his wife, and marry another, committeth adultery against her. 12 And if a woman shall put away her husband, and be married to another, she committeth adultery.
10:14 Suffer the little children to come unto **ME**, and forbid them not; for such is the **Kingdom of GOD**. 15 Verily **I** say unto you, Whosoever shall not receive the **Kingdom of GOD** as a little child, he shall not enter therein.

10:18 Why callest thou **ME** good? none good but **ONE, GOD**. 19 Thou knowest the **Commandments**, Do not commit adultery, Do not kill, Do not steal, Do not bear false witness, Defraud not, Honor thy father and mother.

10:21 One thing thou lackest: go thy way, sell whatsoever thou hast, and give to the poor, and thou shalt have treasure in Heaven: and come, take up your cross, and follow **ME**,

10:23 How hardly shall they that have riches enter into the **Kingdom of GOD**! 24 Children, how hard is it for them that trust in riches to enter into the **Kingdom of GOD**! 25 It is easier for a camel to go through the eye of a needle, than for a rich man to enter into the **Kingdom of GOD**.

10:27 With men impossible, but not with **GOD**: for with **GOD** all things are possible.

10:29 Verily **I** say unto you, There is no man that hath left house, or brethren, or sisters, or mother, or wife, or children, or lands, for **MY** sake, and the **Gospel's**, 30 But he shall receive a hundredfold now in his time, houses, and brethren, and sisters, and mothers, and children, and lands, with persecutions; and in the world to come eternal life. 31 But many first shall be last; and the last first.

10:33 Behold, we go up to Jerusalem; and the **SON of MAN** shall be delivered unto the chief priests, and unto the scribes; and they shall condemn **HIM** to death, and shall deliver **HIM** to the Gentiles: 34 And they shall mock **HIM**, and shall scourge **HIM**, and shall spit upon **HIM**, and shall kill **HIM**; and the third day **HE** shall rise again.

10:36 What would ye that **I** should do for you?

10:38 Ye know not what ye ask: can ye drink of the cup that **I** drink of? and be baptized with the baptism that **I AM** baptized with? 39 Ye shall indeed drink of the cup that **I** drink of: and with the baptism that **I AM** baptized withal shall ye be baptized: 40 But to sit on **MY** right hand and on **MY** left hand is not **MINE** to give; but for whom it is prepared.

10:42 Ye know that they which are accounted to rule over the Gentiles exercise lordship over them; and their great ones exercise authority upon them. 43 But so shall it not among you: but whosoever shall be great among you, shall be your minister: 44 And whosoever of you will be the chiefest, shall be servant to all. 45 For even the **SON of MAN**

came not to be ministered unto, but to minister, and give **HIS** life a ransom for many.
10:51 What wilt thou that **I** should do unto thee? 52 Go thy way; thy faith hath made thee whole.

11:2 Go your way into the village over against you: and as soon as you be entered into it, ye shall find a colt tied, whereon never a man sat; loose him, and bring. 3 And if any man say unto you, Why do ye this? say ye that the **LORD** hath need of him: and straightway he will send him hither.
11:14 No man eat fruit of thee hereafter forever.
11:17 Is it not written, **MY House** shall be called of all nations the **House of Prayer**? but ye have made it a den of thieves.
11:22 Have faith in **GOD**. 23 For verily **I** say unto you, That whosoever shall say unto this mountain, Be thou removed, and be thou cast into the sea; and shall not doubt in his heart, but shall believe that those things which he saith shall come to pass; he shall have whatsoever he saith. 24 Therefore **I** say unto you, What things soever ye desire, when ye pray, believe that ye receive, and ye shall have. 25 And when ye stand praying, forgive, if ye have aught against any, that your **FATHER** also which is in **Heaven** may forgive you your trespasses. 26 But if ye do not forgive, neither will your **FATHER** which is in **Heaven** forgive your trespasses.
11:29 **I** will also ask of you one question, and answer **ME**, and **I** will tell you by what authority **I** do these things. 30 The baptism of John, was from Heaven, or of men? answer **ME**?
11:33 Neither **I** tell you by what authority **I** do these things.

12:1 A man planted a vineyard, and set a hedge about, and digged the wine vat, and built a tower, and let it out to husbandmen, and went into a far country. 2 And at the season he sent to the husbandmen a servant, that he might receive from the husbandmen of the fruit of the vineyard. 3 And they caught, and beat him, and sent him away empty. 4 And again he sent unto them another servant; and at him they cast stones, and wounded in the head, and sent away shamefully handled. 5 And again he sent another; and him they killed, and many others; beating some, and killing some. 6 Having yet therefore one son, his wellbeloved, he sent him also last unto them, saying, They will reverence my son. 7 But those husbandmen said among themselves, This is the heir, come, let us kill him, and the inheritance shall be ours. 8 And they took him, and killed, and cast out of the vineyard. 9 What shall therefore the lord of the vineyard do? he will come and destroy the husbandmen, and will give the vineyard unto others. 10 And have ye not read this Scripture; **The STONE** which the builders rejected is become the **Head of the Corner**: 11 this was the **LORD's** doing, and it is marvelous in our eyes? **12:15** Why tempt ye **ME**? bring **ME** a penny, that **I** may see. 16 Whose this image and superscription? 17 Render to Caesar the things of Caesar's, and to **GOD** the things that are **GOD's**.

12:24 Do ye not therefore err, because ye know not the Scriptures, neither the **Power** of **GOD**? 25 For when they shall rise from the dead, they neither marry, nor are given in marriage; but are as the angels which are in Heaven. 26 And as touching the dead, that they rise; have ye not read in the book of Moses, how in the bush **GOD** spake unto him, saying, **I** the **GOD** of Abraham, and the **GOD** of Isaac, and the **GOD** of Jacob? 27 **HE** is not the **GOD** of the dead, but the **GOD** of the living: ye therefore do greatly err.

12:29 The first of all the **Commandments**, Hear O Israel; The **LORD** our **GOD** is **ONE LORD**: 30 And thou shalt love the **LORD** thy **GOD** with all thy heart, and with all thy soul, and with all thy mind, and with all thy strength: this the first **Commandment**. 31 And the second like, this, Thou shalt love thy neighbor as thyself. There is none other **Commandment** greater than these.

12:35 Thou art not far from the **Kingdom of GOD**. 35 How say the scribes that **CHRIST** is the son of David? 36 For David himself said by the **HOLY GHOST,** The **LORD** said to my **LORD**, Sit **THOU** on **MY** right hand, till **I** make **THINE** enemies **THY** footstool. 37 David therefore himself calleth **HIM LORD**; and whence is **HE** his son? 38 Beware of the scribes, which love to go in long clothing, and salutations in the market places, 39 And the chief seats in the synagogues, and the uppermost rooms at feasts: 40 Which devour widow's houses, and for a pretense make long prayers: these shall receive greater damnation.

12:43 Verily I say unto you, That this poor widow hast cast more in, than all they which have cast into the treasury: 44 For all did cast in of their abundance; but she of her want did cast in all that she had, all her living.

13:2 Seest thou these great buildings? there shall not be left one stone upon another, that shall not be thrown down.
13:5 Take heed lest any deceive you: 6 For many shall come in **MY NAME**, saying, I am; and shall deceive many. 7 And when ye shall hear of wars and rumors of wars, be ye not troubled: for must needs be; but the end not yet. 8 For nation shall rise against nation, and kingdom against kingdom: and there shall be earthquakes in divers places, and there shall be famines and troubles: these the beginning of sorrows. 9 But take heed to yourselves: for they shall deliver you up to councils; and in the synagogues ye shall be beaten: and ye shall be brought before rulers and kings for **MY** sake, for a testimony against them. 10 And the **GOSPEL** must first be published among all nations. 11 But when they shall lead, and deliver you up, take no thought beforehand what ye shall speak, neither do ye premeditate: but whatsoever shall be given you in that hour, that shall ye speak: for it is not ye that speak, but the **HOLY GHOST.** 12 Now the brother shall betray the brother to death, and the father the son; and children shall rise up against parents, and shall cause them to be put to death. 13 And ye shall be hated of all for **MY NAME's** sake: but he that shall endure unto the end, the same shall be saved. 14 But when ye shall see the abomination of desolation, spoken of by Daniel the prophet, standing where it ought not, then let them that be in Judea flee to the mountains: 15 And let not him that is on the housetop not go down into the house, neither enter, to take anything out of his house: 16 And let him that is in the field not turn back again for to take up his garment. 17 But woe unto them that are with child, and to them that give suck in those days! 18 And pray ye that your flight be not in winter. 19 For those days shall be affliction such as was not from the beginning of creation which **GOD** created unto this time, neither shall be. 20 And except that the **LORD** had shortened those days, no flesh should be saved: but for the elect's sake, whom **HE** hath chosen,

HE hath shortened the days. 21 And then if any man shall say to you, Lo, here **CHRIST**, or, lo, there, believe not. 22 For false christs and false prophets shall rise, and shall show signs and wonders, to seduce, if possible, even the elect. 23 But take ye heed: behold, **I** have foretold you all things. 24 But in those days, after that tribulation, the sun shall be darkened, and the moon shall not give her light, 25 And the stars of **Heaven** shall fall, and the powers that are in Heaven shall be shaken. 26 And then shall they see the **SON of MAN** coming in the clouds with great **POWER** and **GLORY**. 27 And then shall **HE** send **HIS** angels, and shall gather together **HIS** elect from the four winds, from the uttermost part of the Earth to the uttermost part of **Heaven**. 28 Now learn a parable of the fig tree: When her branch is yet tender, and putteth forth leaves, ye know that summer is near: 29 So ye in like manner, when ye shall see these things come to pass, know that it is nigh, at the doors. 30 Verily **I** say unto you, That this generation shall not pass, till all these things be done. 31 **Heaven** and **Earth** shall pass away: but **MY WORDS** shall not pass away. 32 But of that day and hour knoweth no man, no, not the angels which are in **Heaven**, neither the **SON**, but the **FATHER**. 33 Take ye heed, watch and pray! for ye know not when the time is. 34 As a man taking a far journey, who left his house, and gave authority to his servants, and to every man his work, and commanded the porter to watch. 35 Watch ye therefore: for ye know not when the master of the house cometh, at even, or at midnight, or at the cockcrowing, or in the morning: 36 Lest coming suddenly he find you sleeping. 37 And what **I** say unto you. **I** say unto all. Watch.

14:6 Let her alone; why trouble ye her? she hath wrought a good work on **ME**. 7 For ye have the poor with you always, and whensoever ye will ye may do them good: but **ME** ye have not always. 8 She hath done what she could: she is come aforehand to anoint **MY** body to the burying. 9 Verily **I** say unto you, Wheresoever this **GOSPEL** shall be preached throughout the whole world, also that she hath done shall be spoken of for a memorial of her.
14:13 Go ye into the city, and there shall meet you a man bearing a pitcher of water: follow him. 14 And wheresoever he shall go in, say

ye to the goodman of the house, The **MASTER** saith, Where is the guest chamber, where **I** shall eat the Passover with **MY** disciples? 15 And he will show you a large upper room furnished prepared: there make ready for us.

14:18 Verily **I** say unto you, One of you which eateth with **ME** shall betray **ME**.

14:20 One of the twelve, that dippeth with **ME** in the dish. 21 The **SON of MAN** indeed goeth, as it is written of **HIM**: but woe to that man by whom the **SON of MAN** is betrayed! good were it for that man if he had never been born. 22 Take, eat; this is **MY** body.

14:24 This is **MY Blood of the New Testament**, which is shed for many. 25 Verily **I** say unto you, **I** will drink no more of the fruit of the vine, until that day that **I** drink it new in the **Kingdom of GOD**.

14:27 All ye shall be offended because of **ME** this night: for it is written, I will smite the **SHEPHERD**, and the sheep shall be scattered. 28 But after that **I AM** risen, I will go before you into Galilee.

14:30 Verily **I** say unto thee, That this day, in the night, before the cock crow twice, thou shalt deny **ME** thrice.

14:32 Sit ye here, while **I** shall pray.

14:34 MY soul is exceeding sorrowful unto death: tarry ye here, and watch.

14:36 ABBA, FATHER, all things possible unto **THEE**; take away this cup from **ME**! nevertheless, not what **I** will, but what **THOU** wilt. 37 Simon, sleepest thou? couldest not thou watch one hour? 38 Watch ye and pray, lest ye enter into temptation. The spirit truly ready, but the flesh weak.

14:41 Sleep on now, and take rest: it is enough, the hour is come; behold, the **SON of MAN** is betrayed into the hands of sinners. 42 Rise up, let us go; lo, he that betrayeth **ME** is at hand.

14:48 Are ye come out, as against a thief, with swords and staves to take **ME**? 49 **I** was daily with you in the temple teaching, and ye took **ME** not: but the Scriptures must be fulfilled.

14:62 I AM: and ye shall see the **SON of MAN** sitting on the right hand of **POWER**, and coming in the clouds of Heaven.

14:72 Before the cock crow twice, thou shalt deny **ME** thrice.

15:2 Thou sayest.
15:34 E'LO-I, E'LO-I, lama sabach'thani? **MY GOD, MY GOD,** why hast **THOU** forsaken **ME**?

16:15 Go ye into all the world, and preach the **GOSPEL** to every creature. 16 He that believeth and is baptized shall be saved; be he that believeth not shall be damned. 17 And these signs shall follow them that believe; In **MY NAME** shall they cast out devils; they shall speak with new tongues; 18 They shall take up serpents; and if they drink any deadly thing, it shall not hurt them; they shall lay hands on the sick, and they shall recover.

What JESUS Said

LUKE

2:49 How is it that ye sought **ME?** wist ye not that **I** must be about **MY FATHER's** business?

4:4 It is written, That man shall not live by bread alone, but by every **WORD** of **GOD.**
4:8 Get thee behind **ME** Satan: for it is written, Thou shalt worship the **LORD** thy **GOD,** and **HIM** only shalt thou serve.
4:12 It is said, Thou shalt not tempt the **LORD** thy **GOD.**
4:18 The **SPIRIT** of the **LORD** upon **ME**, because **HE** hath anointed **ME** to preach the **GOSPEL** to the poor; **HE** hath sent **ME** to heal the brokenhearted, to preach deliverance to the captives, and recovering of sight to the blind, to set at liberty them that are bruised, 19 To preach the acceptable year of the **LORD.**
4:21 This day is this Scripture fulfilled in your ears.
4:23 Ye will surely say unto **ME** this proverb, Physician, heal thyself: whatsoever we have heard done in Capernaum, do also here in **THY** country. 24 Verily **I** say unto you, No prophet is accepted in his own country. 25 But **I** tell you of a truth, many widows were in Israel in the days of Elias, when the Heaven was shut up three years and six months, when great famine was throughout all the land; 26 But unto none of them was Elias sent, save unto Sarepta, of Sidon, unto a woman a widow. 27 And many lepers were in Israel in the time of Eliseus the prophet: and none of them was cleansed, saving Naaman the Syrian.
4:35 Hold thy peace, and come out of him.
4:43 **I** must preach the **Kingdom of GOD** to other cities also: for therefore am **I** sent.

5:4 Launch out into the deep, and let down your nets for a draught.
5:10 Fear not; from henceforth thou shalt catch men.
5:13 **I** will: be thou clean. 14 but go, and show thyself to the priest, and offer for thine cleansing, according as Moses commanded, for a testimony unto them.
5:20 Man, thy sins are forgiven thee.
5:22 What reason ye in your hearts? 23 Whether is easier, to say, Thy sins be forgiven thee; or to say, Rise up and walk? 24 But that ye know

that the **SON of MAN** hath power upon Earth to forgive sins, **I** say unto thee, Arise, and take up thy couch, and go into thine house.
5:27 Follow **ME**.
5:31 They that are whole need not a physician; but they that are sick. 32 I came not to call the righteous, but sinners to repentance.
5:34 Can ye make the children of the bridechamber fast, while the bridegroom is with them? 35 But the days will come, when the bridegroom shall be taken away from them and then shall they fast in those days. 36 No man putteth a piece of a new garment upon an old; if otherwise, then both the new maketh a rent, and the piece that was out of the new agreeth not with the old. 37 And no man putteth new wine into old bottles; else the new wine will burst the bottles, and be spilled, and the bottles shall perish. 38 But new wine must be put into new bottles; and both are preserved. 39 No man also having drunk old straightway desireth new; for he saith, The old is better.

6:3 Have ye not read so much as this, what David did, when himself was ahungered, and they which were with him; 4 How he went into the House of **GOD**, and did take and eat the showbread, and gave also to them that was with him: which it is unlawful to eat but for the priests alone? 5 And the **SON of MAN** is **LORD** also of the sabbath. **6:8** Rise up, and stand forth in the midst. 9 **I** will ask you one thing; is it lawful on the sabbath days to do good or to do evil? to save life, or to destroy? 10 Stretch forth thy hand.
6:20 Blessed poor: for yours is the **Kingdom of GOD**. 21 Blessed that hunger now: for ye shall be filled, Blessed that weep now: for ye shall laugh. 22 Blessed are ye, when men shall hate you, and when they shall seperate you, and shall reproach, and cast your name as evil, for the **SON of MAN's** sake. 23 Rejoice ye in that day, and leap for joy: for, behold, your reward great in **Heaven**: for in like manner did their fathers unto the prophets. 24 But woe unto you that are rich: for ye have received your consolation. 25 Woe unto you that are full! for ye shall hunger. Woe unto you that laugh now! for ye shall mourn and weep. 26 Woe unto you, when all men shall speak well of you! for so did their fathers to the false prophets. 27 But **I** say unto you which hear, Love

your enemies, do good to them which hate you, 28 Bless them that curse you, and pray for them which despitefully use you. 29 And unto him that smiteth thee on the cheek offer also the other; and of him that taketh away thy cloak forbid not coat also. 30 Give to every man that asked of thee; and of him that taketh away thy goods ask not again. 31 And as ye would that men should do to you, do ye also to them likewise. 32 For if ye love them which love you, what thank have ye? for sinners also love those that love them. 33 And if ye do good to them which do good to you, what thank have ye? for sinners also do even the same. 34 And if you lend of whom ye hope to receive, what thank have ye? for sinners also lend to sinners, to receive as much again. 35 But love your enemies, and do good, and lend, hoping for nothing again; and your reward shall be great, and ye shall be the children of the **HIGHEST**: for **HE** is kind unto the unthankful and the evil. 36 Be ye therefore merciful, as your **FATHER** also is merciful. 37 Judge not, and ye shall not be judged: condemn not, and ye shall not be condemned: forgive, and ye shall be forgiven: 38 Give, and it shall be given unto you; good measure, pressed down, and shaken together, and running over, shall men give into your bosom. For with the same measure that ye mete withal it shall be measured to you again. 39 Can the blind lead the blind? shall they not both fall into the ditch? 40 The disciple is not above his master: but every one that is perfect shall be as his master. 41 And why beholdest thou the mote that is in thy brother's eye, but perceivest not the beam that is in thine own eye? 42 Either how canst thou say to thy brother, Brother, let me pull out the mote that is in thine eye, when thou thyself beholdest not the beam that is in thine own eye? Thou hypocrite, cast out first the beam out of thine own eye, and then shalt thou see clearly to pull out the mote that is in thy brother's eye. 43 For a good tree bringeth not forth corrupt fruit; neither doth a corrupt tree bring forth good fruit. 44 For every tree is known by his own fruit. For a thorns men do not gather figs, nor of a bramble bush gather they grapes. 45 A good man out of the good treasure of his heart bringeth forth that which is good; and an evil man out of the evil treasure of his heart bringeth forth that which is evil: for of the abundance of the heart his mouth speaketh. 46 And why call **ME**, **LORD**, **LORD**, and do not the things which **I** say? 47 Whosoever cometh to **ME**, and heareth **MY** sayings, and doeth them, **I** will show you to whom he is like: 48 He is like a man which built a house, and digged deep, and laid the foundation on a **Rock**: and when the flood arose, the stream beat vehemently upon that house, and could not shake it; for it was founded upon a **Rock**. 49 But he that heareth, and doeth not, is like a man that without a foundation built a house upon the earth; against which the stream did beat vehemently, and immediately it fell; and the ruin of that house was great.

7:9 I say unto you, **I** have not found so great faith, no, not in Israel.
7:13 Weep not. 14 Young man, **I** say unto thee, Arise.
7:22 Go your way, and tell John what things ye have seen and heard; how that the blind see, the lame walk, the lepers are cleansed, the deaf hear, the dead is raised, to the poor the **GOSPEL** is preached. 23 And blessed is, whosoever shall not be offended in **ME**. 24 What went ye out into the wilderness for to see? A reed shaken with the wind? 25 But what went ye out to see? A man clothed in soft raiment? Behold, they which are gorgeously apparelled, and live delicately, are in king's courts. 26 But what went ye out for to see? A prophet? Yea, **I** say unto you, and much more than a prophet. 27 This is, of whom it is written, Behold, **I** send **MY** messenger before **THY** face, which shall prepare **THY** way before **THEE**. 28 For **I** say unto you, Among those that are born of women there is not a greater prophet than John the Baptist: but he is least in the **Kingdom of GOD** is greater than he.
7:31 Whereunto then shall **I** liken the men of this generation? and to what are they like? 32 They are like unto children sitting in the market place, and calling one to another, and saying; We have piped unto you, and ye have not danced; we have mourned to you, and ye have not wept. 33 For John the Baptist came neither eating bread nor drinking wine; and ye say, He hath a devil. 34 The **SON of MAN** is come eating and drinking; and ye say, Behold a gluttonous man, and a winebibber, a friend of publicans and sinners! 35 But wisdom is justified of all her children.
7:40 Simon, **I** have somewhat to say unto thee. 41 There was a certain creditor which had two debtors: the one owed five hundred pence, and

the other fifty. 42 And when they had nothing to pay, he frankly forgave them both. Tell **ME** therefore, which of them will love him most? 43 Thou hast rightly judged. 44 Seest thou this woman? **I** entered into thine house, thou gavest **ME** no water for **MY** feet: but she hath washed **MY** feet with tears, and wiped with the hairs of her head. 45 Thou gavest **ME** no kiss: but this woman, since the time **I** came in, hath not ceased to kiss **MY** feet. 46 **MY** head with oil thou didst not anoint: but this woman hast anointed **MY** feet with ointment. 47 Wherefore **I** say unto thee, Her sins, which are many, are forgiven, for she loved much: but to whom little is forgiven, loveth little. 48 Thy sins are forgiven. **7:50** Thy faith hath saved thee; go in peace.

8:5 A sower went out to sow his **SEED**: and as he sowed, **SOME** fell by the wayside; and it was trodden down, and the fowls of the air devoured it. 6 And **SOME** fell upon a rock; and as soon as it was sprung up, it withered away because it lacked moisture. 7 And **SOME** fell among thorns; and the thorns sprang up with it, and choked it. 8 And **OTHER** fell on good ground, and sprang up, and bare fruit a hundredfold. He that hath ears to hear, let him hear.
8:10 Unto you it is given to know the mysteries of the **Kingdom of GOD**: but to others in parables; that seeing they might not see, and hearing they might not understand. 11 Now the parable is this: **THE SEED** is the **WORD of GOD**. 12 Those by the wayside are they that hear; then cometh the devil, and taketh away the **WORD** out of their hearts, lest they should believe and be saved. 13 They on the rock, which, when they hear, receive the **WORD** with joy; and these have no root, which for a while believe, and in time of temptation fall away. 14 And that which fell among the thorns are they, which, when they have heard, go forth, and are choked, with cares and riches and pleasures of life, and bring no fruit to perfection. 15 But that on the good ground are they, which in an honest and good heart, having heard the **WORD**, keep, and bring forth fruit with patience. 16 No man, when he hath lighted a candle, covereth it with a vessel, or putteth under a bed; but setteth on a candlestick, that they which enter in may see the light. 17 For nothing is secret, that shall not be made manifest; neither hid, that

shall not be known and come abroad. 18 Take heed therefore how ye hear: for whosoever hath, to him shall be given; and whosoever hath not, from him shall be taken even that which he seemeth to have.

8:21 **MY** mother and **MY** brethren are these which hear the **WORD of GOD**, and do it. 22 Let us go over unto the other side of the lake.

8:25 Where is thy faith?

8:30 What is thy name?

8:39 Return to thine own house, and show how great things **GOD** hath done unto thee.

8:45 Who touched **ME**? Who touched **ME**? 46 Somebody hath touched **ME**: for **I** perceive that virtue is gone out of **ME**.

8:48 Daughter, be of good comfort: thy faith hath made thee whole; go in peace.

8:50 Fear not: believe only, and she shall be made whole.

8:52 Weep not; she is not dead, but sleepeth.

8:54 Maid, arise.

9:3 Take nothing for the journey, neither staves, nor scrip, neither bread, neither money; neither have two coats apiece. 4 And whatsoever house ye enter into, there abide, and thence depart. 5 And whosoever will not receive you, when ye go out of that city, shake off the very dust from your feet for a testimony against them.

9:13 Give ye them to eat. 14 Make them sit down by fifties in a company.

9:18 Whom say the people that **I AM**?

9:20 But whom say ye that **I AM**?

9:22 The **SON of MAN** must suffer many things, and be rejected of the elders and chief priests and scribes, and be slain, and be raised the third day. 23 If any will come after **ME**, let him deny himself, and take up his cross daily, and follow **ME**. 24 For whosoever will save his life shall lose it: whosoever will lose his life for **MY** sake, the same shall save it. 25 For what is a man advantaged, if he gain the whole world, and lose himself, or be cast away? 26 For whosoever shall be ashamed of **ME** and of **MY WORDS**, of him shall the **SON of MAN** be ashamed, when **HE** shall come in **HIS** own **GLORY**, and **FATHER's**, and of the holy angels. 27 But **I** tell you of a truth, there be some standing here, which shall not taste of death, till they see the **Kingdom of GOD**.

9:41 O faithless and perverse generation, how long shall **I** be with you, and suffer you? Bring thy son hither.

9:44 Let these sayings sink down into your ears: for the **SON of MAN** shall be delivered into the hands of men.

9:48 Whosoever shall receive this child in **MY NAME** receiveth **ME**; and whosoever shall receive **ME**, receiveth **HIM** that sent **ME**: for he that is least among you all, the same shall be great.

9:50 Forbid not: for he that is not against us is for us.

9:55 Ye know not what manner of spirit ye are of. For the **SON of MAN** is not come to destroy men's lives, but to save.

9:58 Foxes have holes, and birds of the air nests; but the **SON of MAN** hath no where to lay head. 59 Follow **ME**. 60 Let the dead bury their dead: but go thou and preach the **Kingdom of GOD**.

9:62 No man, having put his hand to the plow, and looking back, is fit for the **Kingdom of GOD**.

10:2 The harvest truly great, but the laborers few: pray ye therefore the **LORD** of the harvest, that **HE** would send forth laborers into **HIS** harvest. 3 Go your ways: behold, **I** send you forth as lambs among wolves. 4 Carry neither purse, nor scrip, nor shoes: and salute no man by the way. 5 And into whatsoever house ye enter, first say, Peace to this house. 6 And if the **SON of PEACE** be there, your peace shall rest upon it: if not, it shall turn to you again. 7 And in the same house remain, eating and drinking such things as they give: for the laborer is worthy of his hire. Go not from house to house. 8 And into whatever city ye enter, and they receive you, eat such things as are set before you: 9 And heal the sick that are therein, and say unto them, The **Kingdom of GOD** is come nigh unto you. 10 But into whatever city ye enter, and they receive you not, go your ways out into the streets of the same, and say, 11 Even the very dust of your city, which cleaveth on us, we do wipe off against you: notwithstanding, be ye sure of this, that the **Kingdom of GOD** is come nigh unto you. 12 But **I** say unto you, that it shall be more tolerable in that day for Sodom, than for that city. 13 Woe unto thee, Chorazin! woe unto thee, Bethsaida! for if the mighty works had been done in Tyre and Sidon, which had been done in you, they would a great while ago repented, sitting in sackcloth and ashes. 14 But it shall be more tolerable for Tyre and Sidon at the judgement, than for you. 15 And thou Capernaum, which art exalted to Heaven, shalt be thrust down to hell. 16 He that heareth you heareth **ME**; and he that despiseth you despiseth **ME**; and he that despiseth **ME** despiseth **HIM** that sent **ME**. **10:18** I beheld Satan as lightning fall from **Heaven**. 19 Behold, **I** give you power to thread upon serpents and scorpions, and over all the power of the enemy; and nothing by any means hurt you. 20 Notwithstanding, in this rejoice not, that the spirits are subject unto you; but rather rejoice, because your names are written in Heaven. 21 **I** thank **THEE** O **FATHER, LORD of Heaven and Earth**, that **THOU** hast hid these things from the wise and prudent, and hast revealed them among babes: even so, **FATHER**, for so it seemed good in **THY** sight. 22 All things are delivered to **ME** of **MY FATHER**: and no man knoweth who the **SON** is, but the **FATHER**, and who the **FATHER** is, but the **SON**, and to whom the **SON** will reveal. 23 Blessed the eyes which see the things which ye see: 24 For **I** tell you, that many prophets and kings have desired to see those things which ye see, and have not seen; and to hear those things which ye hear, and have not heard.

10:26 What is written in the **LAW**? how readest thou?

10:28 Thou hast answered right: this do, and thou shalt live.

10:30 A certain went down from Jerusalem to Jericho, and fell among thieves, which stripped him of his raiment, and wounded, and departed, leaving half dead. 31 And by chance there came down a certain priest that way; and when he saw him, he passed by on the other side. 32 And likewise a Levite, when he was at the place, came and looked, and passed by on the other side. 33 But a certain Samaritan, as he journeyed, came where he was; and when he saw him, he had compassion, 34 And went to, and bound up his wounds, pouring in oil and wine, and set him on his beast, and brought him to an inn, and took care of him. 35 And on the morrow when he departed, he took out two pence, and gave to the host, and said unto him, Take care of him: and whatsoever thou spendest more, when I come again, I will repay thee. 36 Which now of

these three, thinkest thou, was neighbor unto him that fell among the thieves? 37 Go, and do thou likewise.
10:41 Martha, MARTHA, thou art careful and troubled about many things: 42 But one thing is needful; and Mary hath chosen that good part, which shall not be taken away from her.

11:2 When ye pray, say, Our **FATHER** which art in **Heaven, Hallowed** be **THY NAME. THY Kingdom** come. **THY Will** be done, as in **Heaven,** so in **Earth.** 3 Give us day by day our daily bread. 4 And forgive us our sins; for we also forgive everyone that is indebted to us. And lead us not into temptation, but deliver us from evil. 5 Which of you shall have a friend, and shall go unto him at midnight, and say unto him, Friend, lend me three loaves; 6 For a friend of mine in his journey is come to me, and I have nothing to set before him? 7 And he from within shall answer and say, Trouble me not: the door is now shut, and my children are with me in bed; I cannot rise and give thee. 8 I say unto you, Though he will not rise and give him, because he is his friend, yet because of his importunity he will rise and give as many as he needeth. 9 And **I** say unto you, Ask, and it shall be given you; seek, and ye shall find; knock, and it shall be opened unto you. 10 For everyone that asketh receiveth; and he that seeketh findeth; and him that knocketh it shall be opened. 11 If a son shall ask bread of you that is a father, will he give him a stone? or if a fish, will he for a fish give him a serpent? 12 Or if he shall ask an egg, will he offer him a scorpion? 13 If ye then being evil, know how to give good gifts unto your children; how much more shall the **Heavenly Father** give the **HOLY SPIRIT** to them that ask **HIM**?
11:17 Every kingdom divided against itself is brought to desolation; and a house against a house falleth. 18 If Satan also be divided against himself, how shall his kingdom stand? because ye say that **I** cast out devils through Beelzebub. 19 And if **I** by Beelzebub cast out devils, by whom does your sons cast out? therefore shall they be your judges. 20 But if **I** with the finger of **GOD** cast out devils, no doubt the **Kingdom of GOD** is come upon you. 21 When a strong man armed keepeth his palace, his goods are in peace: 22 But when a stronger than he

shall come upon him, and overcome him, he taketh away all his armor wherein he trusted, and divedeth his spoils. 23 He that is not with **ME** is against **ME**; and he that gathereth not with **ME** scattereth. 24 When the unclean spirit is gone out of a man, he walked through dry places, seeking rest; and finding none, he saith, I will return unto my house whence I came out. 25 And when he cometh, he findeth swept and garnished. 26 Then goeth he, and taketh seven other spirits more wicked than himself, and they enter in, and dwell there: and the last of the man is worse than the first.

11:28 Yea, rather, blessed they that hear the **WORD of GOD**, and keep **IT**. 29 This is an evil generation: they seek a sign; and there shall no sign be given it, but the sign of Jonah the prophet. 30 For as Jonah was a sign unto the Ninevites, so shall the **SON of MAN** be to this generation. 31 The queen of the south shall rise up in the judgement with the men of this generation, and condemn them: for she came from the utmost parts of the Earth to hear the wisdom of Solomon; and, behold, a **Greater** than Solomon here. 32 The men of Nineveh shall rise up in the judgement with this generation, and shall condemn it: for they repented at the preaching of Jonah; and, behold, a **Greater** than Jonah here. 33 No man, when he hath lighted a candle, putteth in a secret place, neither under a bushel, but on a candlestick, that they that come in may see the light. 34 The light of the body is the eye: therefore when the eye is single, thy whole body also is full of light; but when is evil, thy body also is full of darkness. 35 Take heed therefore, that the light which is in thee be not darkness. 36 If thy whole body therefore full of light, having no part dark, the whole shall be full of light, as when the bright shining of a candle doth give thee light.

11:39 Now do you Pharisees make clean the outside of the cup and platter; but your inward part is full of ravening and wickedness. 40 Fools, did not **HE**, that made that which is without, make that which is within also? 41 But rather give alms of such things as ye have; and, behold, all things are clean unto you. 42 But woe unto you Pharisees! for ye tithe mint and rue and all manner of herbs, and pass over **Judgement** and **Love of GOD**: these ought ye to have done, and not to leave the other undone. 43 Woe unto you, Pharisees! for ye love the uppermost seats in the synagogues, and greetings in the markets. 44 Woe unto you, scribes and Pharisees, hypocrites! for ye are as graves which appear not, and the men that walk over are not aware.

11:46 Woe unto you also, ye lawyers! for ye lade men with burdens grievous to be borne, and ye yourselves touch not the burdens with one of your fingers. 47 Woe unto you! for ye build sepulchres of the prophets, and your fathers killed them. 48 Truly ye bear witness that ye allow the deeds of your fathers: for they indeed killed them, and ye build their sepulchres. 49 Therefore also said the **Wisdom of GOD, I** will send them prophets and apostles, and of them they shall slay and persecute: 50 That the blood of all the prophets, which was shed from the foundation of the world, may be required of this generation. 51 From the blood of Abel unto the blood of Zechariah, which perished between the altar and the temple: verily **I** say unto you, It shall be required of this generation. 52 Woe unto you, lawyers! for ye have taken away the key of knowledge: ye entered not in yourselves; and them that were entering in ye hindered.

12:1 Beware ye of the leaven of the Pharisees, which is hypocrisy. 2 For there is nothing covered, that shall not be revealed; neither hid, that shall not be known. 3 Therefore, whatsoever ye have spoken in darkness shall be heard in the light; and that which ye have spoken in the ear in closets shall be proclaimed upon the housetops. 4 And **I** say unto you **MY** friends, Be not afraid of them that kill the body, and after that have no more that they can do. 5 But **I** will forewarn you **WHOM** ye shall fear. Fear **HIM**, which after **HE** hath killed hath power to cast into hell; yea **I** say unto you, Fear **HIM**. 6 Are not five sparrows sold for two farthings, and not one of them is forgotten before **GOD**? 7 But even the very hairs of your head are all numbered. Fear not therefore: ye are more value than many sparrows. 8 Also **I** say unto you, Whosoever shall confess **ME** before men, him shall the **SON of MAN** also confess before the angels of **GOD**: 9 But he that denieth **ME** before men shall be denied before the angels of **GOD**. 10 And whosoever shall speak a word against the **SON of MAN**, it shall be forgiven him: but unto him that blasphemeth against the **HOLY GHOST** it shall not be forgiven. 11 And when they bring you into the synagogues, and magistrates, and powers, take ye no thought how or what thing ye shall answer, or what ye shall say: 12 For the **HOLY GHOST** shall teach you in the same hour what ye ought to say.

12:14 Man, who made **ME** a judge or a divider over you? 15 Take heed, and beware of covetousness: for a man's life consisteth not in the abundance of the things which he possesseth. 16 The ground of a certain rich man brought forth plentifully: 17 And he thought within himself, saying, What shall I do, because I have no room where to bestow my fruits? 18 And he said, This will I do: I will pull down my barns, and build greater; and there will I bestow all my fruits and goods. 19 And I will say to my soul, Soul, thou hast much goods laid up for many years; take thine ease, eat, drink, be merry. 20 But **GOD** said unto him, Fool, this night thy soul shall be required of thee: then whose shall those things be; which thou hast provided? 21 So he that layeth up treasure for himself, and is not rich toward **GOD**. 22 Therefore **I** say unto you, Take no thought for your life, what ye shall eat: neither for the body, what ye shall put on. 23 The life is more than meat, and the body than raiment. 24 Consider the ravens: for they neither sow nor reap; which neither have storehouse or barns; and **GOD** feedeth them: how much more are ye better than the fowls? 25 And which of you with taking thought can add to his stature one cubit? 26 If ye then be not able to do that thing which is least, why take ye thought for the rest? 27 Consider the lilies and how they grow: they toil not, they spin not; and yet **I** say unto you, that Solomon in all his glory was not arrayed like one of these. 28 If then **GOD** so clothe the grass, which is today in the field, and tomorrow cast into the oven; how much more you, O ye with little faith? 29 And seek not ye what ye shall eat, or what ye shall drink, neither be ye of doubtful mind. 30 For all these things do the nations of the world seek after: and your **FATHER** knoweth that ye have need of these things. 31 But rather seek ye the **Kingdom of GOD**: and all these things shall be added unto you. 32 Fear not, little flocks; for it is your **FATHER's** good pleasure to give you the **Kingdom**. 33 Sell that ye have, and give alms; provide yourselves bags which wax not old, a treasure in the **Heavens** that faileth not, where no thief approacheth, neither moth corrupted. 34 For where your treasure is, there will your heart be also. 35 Let your loins be girded about, and lights burning; 36

And ye yourselves like unto men that wait for their lord, when he will return from the wedding; that, when he cometh and knocketh, they may open unto him immediately. 37 Blessed those servants, whom the **LORD** when **HE** cometh shall find watching: Verily **I** say unto you, that **HE** shall gird **HIMSELF**, and make them to sit down to meat, and will come forth and serve them. 38 And if **HE** shall come in the second watch or come in the third watch, and find so, blessed are those servants. 39 And this know, that if the goodman of the house had known what hour the thief would come, he would have watched, and not have suffered his house to be broken through. 40 Be ye therefore ready also: for the **SON of MAN** cometh at an hour when ye think not. **12:42** Who then is that faithful and wise steward, whom **LORD** shall make ruler over **HIS** household, to give portion of meat in due season? 43 Blessed that servant, whom his **LORD** when **HE** cometh shall find so doing. 44 Of a truth **I** say unto you, That **HE** will make him ruler over all that **HE** hath. 45 But and if that servant say in his heart, my **LORD** delayeth **HIS** coming; and shall begin to beat the menservants and maidens, and to eat and drink, and to be drunken; 46 The **LORD** of that servant will come in a day when he looketh not for, and at an hour when he is not aware, and will cut him in sunder, and will appoint him his portion with the unbelievers. 47 And that servant, which knew his **LORD's Will**, and prepared not, neither did according to **HIS Will**, shall be beaten with many. 48 But he that knew not, and did commit things worthy of stripes, shall be beaten with few. For unto whomsoever much is given, of him shall be much required; and to him men have committed much, of him they will ask the more. 49 **I AM** come to send fire on the Earth; and what will **I**, if it be already kindled? 50 But **I** have a baptism to be baptized with; and how am **I** straitened till it is accomplished! 51 Suppose ye that **I AM** come to give peace on Earth? **I** tell you, Nay; but rather division: 52 For from henceforth there shall be five in one house divided, three against two, and two against three. 53 The father shall be divided against the son, and the son against the father; the mother against the daughter, and the daughter against the mother; the mother-in-law against her daughter-in-law, and the daughter-in-law against her mother-in-law. 54 When ye see a cloud rise out of the west, straightway ye say, There cometh a shower; and so it is. 55 And when the south wind blow, ye say, There will be heat; and it cometh to pass. 56 Hypocrites, ye can discern the face of the sky and of the Earth; but how is it that ye do not discern this time? 57 Yea, and why even of yourselves judge ye not what is right? 58 When thou goest with thine adversary to the magistrate, in the way, give diligence that thou mayest be delivered from him; lest he hale thee to the officer, and the officer cast thee in prison. 59 **I** tell thee, thou shalt not depart thence, till thou hast paid the very last mite.

13:2 Suppose ye that those Galileans were sinners above all the Galileans, because they suffered such things? 3 **I** tell you, Nay: but, except ye repent, ye shall all likewise perish. 4 Or those eighteen, upon whom the tower of Siloam fell, and slew them, think ye that they were sinners above all men that dwelt in Jerusalem? 5 **I** tell you, Nay: but except ye repent, ye shall all likewise perish. 6 A certain had a fig tree planted in his vineyard; and he came and sought fruit thereon, and found none. 7 Then said he unto the dresser of his vineyard, Behold, these three years I come seeking fruit on this fig tree, and found none: cut it down; why cumbereth it the ground? 8 And he answering said unto him, Lord, let it alone this year also, till I shall dig about it, and dung: 9 And if it bear fruit, and if not, after that thou shalt cut it down.
13:12 Woman, thou art loosed from thine infirmity.
13:15 Hypocrite, doth not each one of you on the sabbath loose his ox or ass from the stall, and lead away to watering? 16 And ought not this woman, being a daughter of Abraham, whom Satan hath bound, lo, these eighteen years, be loosed from this bond on the sabbath day?
13:18 Unto what is the **Kingdom of GOD** like? and whereunto shall **I** resemble it? 19 It is like a grain of mustard seed, which a man took, and cast into his garden; and it grew, and waxed a great tree; and the fowls of the air lodged in the branches of it. 20 Whereunto shall **I** liken unto the **Kingdom of GOD**? 21 It is like leaven, which a woman took and hid in three measures of meal, till the whole was leavened.
13:24 Strive to enter in at the strait gate: for many, **I** say unto you, will seek to enter in, and shall not be able. 25 When once the master of the house is risen up, and hath shut the door, and ye begin to stand without,

The Blood of Christ

and to knock at the door, saying, **LORD, LORD,** open unto us, and **HE** shall answer and say unto you, **I** know you not whence ye are; 26 Then shall ye begin to say, We have eaten and drunk in **THY** presence, and **THOU** hast taught in our streets. 27 But **HE** shall say, I tell you, **I** know you not whence ye are; depart from **ME,** all workers of iniquity. 28 There shall be weeping and gnashing of teeth, when ye shall see Abraham, Isaac, and Jacob, and all the prophets, in the **Kingdom of GOD,** and you thrust out. 29 And they shall come from the east, and the west, and from the north, and the south, and shall sit down in the **Kingdom of GOD.** 30 And, behold, there are last which shall be first; and the first shall be last.

13:32 Go ye, and tell that fox, Behold, **I** cast out devils, and **I** do cures today and tomorrow, and the third **I** shall be perfected. 33 Nevertheless I must walk today, and tomorrow, and the following: for it cannot be that a prophet perish out of Jerusalem. 34 O Jerusalem, Jerusalem, which killest the prophets, and stonest them that are sent unto thee; how often **I** would have gathered thy children together, as a hen brood under wings, and ye would not! 35 Behold, your house is left unto you desolate: and verily **I** say unto you, Ye shall not see **ME,** until come when ye shall say, Blessed **HE** that cometh in the **NAME of the LORD.**

14:3 Is it lawful to heal on the sabbath day?
14:5 Which of you shall have an ass or an ox fallen into a pit, and will not straightway pull him out on the sabbath day?
14:8 When thou art bidden of any to a wedding, sit not down in the highest room; lest a more honorable man than thou be bidden of him; 9 And he that bade thee and him come and say to thee, Give this man place; and thou begin with shame to take the lowest room. 10 But when thou art bidden, go and sit down in the lowest room; that when he that bade thee cometh, he may say unto thee, Friend, go up higher: then shall thou have worship in the presence of them that sit at meat with thee. 11 For whosoever exalteth himself shall be abased; and he that humbleth himself shall be exalted. 12 When thou makest a dinner or a supper, call not thy friends, nor thy brethren, neither thy kinsmen, nor rich

neighbors; lest they also bid thee again, and a recompense be made thee. 13 But when thou makest a feast, call the poor, the maimed, the lame, the blind: 14 And thou shalt be blessed; for they cannot recompense thee: for thou shalt be recompensed at the resurrection of the just.

14:16 A certain man made a great supper, and bade many: 17 And sent his servant at supper time to say to them that were bidden, Come, for all things are now ready. 18 And they all with one began to make excuse. The first say unto him, I have brought a piece of ground, and I must needs go and see it: I pray thee have me excused. 19 And another said, I have bought five yoke of oxen, and I go to prove them: I pray thee have me excused. 20 And another said, I have married a wife, and therefore I cannot come. 21 So that servant came, and showed his lord these things. Then the master of the house being angry said to his servant, Go out quickly unto the streets and lanes of the city, and bring hither the poor, and the maimed, and the halt, and the blind. 22 And the servant said, Lord, it is done as thou hast commanded, and yet there is room. 23 And the lord said unto the servant, Go out into the highways and hedges, and compel to come in, that my house may be filled. 24 For I say unto you, That none of those men which were bidden shall taste of my supper.

14:26 If any come to **ME**, and hate not his father, and mother, and wife, and children, and brethren, and sisters, yea, and his own life also, he cannot be **MY** disciple. 27 And whosoever doth not bear his cross, and come after **ME**, cannot be **MY** disciple. 28 For which of you, intending to build a tower, sitteth not down first, and counteth the cost, whether he have to finish? 29 Lest haply, after he hath laid the foundation, and is not able to finish, all that behold begin to mock him, 30 Saying, This man began to build, and was not able to finish. 31 Or what king, going to make war against another king, sitteth not down first, and consulteth whether he be able with ten-thousand to meet him that cometh against him with twenty thousand? 32 Or else, while the other is yet, a great way off, he sendeth an ambassage, and desireth conditions of peace. 33 So likewise, whosoever he be of you that forsaketh not all that he hath, he cannot be **MY** disciple. 34 Salt good: but if salt have lost his savor, wherewith shall it be seasoned? 35 It is neither fit for the land, nor yet for the dunghill; men cast it out. He that hath ears to hear, let him hear.

The Blood of Christ

15:4 What man of you, having a hundred sheep, if he lose one of them, doth not leave the ninety and nine in the wilderness, and go after that which is lost, until he find it? 5 And when he hath found, he layeth on his shoulders, rejoicing. 6 And when he cometh home, he calleth together friends and neighbors, saying unto them, Rejoice with me; for I have found my sheep which was lost. 7 **I** say unto you, that likewise joy shall be in **Heaven** over one sinner that repenteth, more than ninety and nine just persons, which need no repentance. 8 Either what woman having ten pieces of silver, if she lose one piece, doth not light a candle and sweep the house, and seek diligently till she find? 9 And when she hath found, she calleth friends and neighbors together, saying, Rejoice with me; for I have found the piece which I had lost. 10 Likewise **I** say unto you, there is joy in the presence of the angels of **GOD** over one sinner that repenteth. 11 A certain man had two sons: 12 And the younger of them said to father, Father, give me the portion of goods that falleth. And he divided unto them living. 13 And not many days after the younger son gathered all together, and took his journey into a far country, and there wasted his substance with riotous living. 14 And when he had spent all, there arose a mighty famine in that land; and he began to be in want. 15 And he went and joined himself to a citizen of that country; and he sent him into his fields to feed swine. 16 And he would fain have filled his belly with the husks that the swine did eat: and no man gave unto him. 17 And when he came to himself, he said, How many hired servants of my father's have bread enough and to spare, and I perish with hunger! 18 I will arise and go to my father and will say unto him, Father, I have sinned against **Heaven**, and before thee, 19 And am no more worthy to be called thy son: make me as one of your hired servants. 20 And he arose, and came to his father. But when he was a great way off, his father saw him, and had compassion, and ran, and fell on his neck, and kissed him. 21 And the son said unto him, Father, I have sinned against **Heaven**, and in thy sight, and am no more worthy to be called thy son. 22 But the father said unto his servants, Bring forth the best robe, and put on him; and put a ring on his hand, and shoes on feet: 23 And bring hither the fatted calf, and kill; and let us eat, and be merry. 24 For this my son was dead, and is alive again; he was lost, and is found. And they began to be merry.

25 Now his elder son was in the field: and he came and drew nigh to the house, he heard music and dancing. 26 And he called one of the servants, and asked what these things meant. 27 And he said unto him, Thy brother is come; and thy father hath killed the fatted calf, because he hath received him safe and sound. 28 And he was angry, and would not go in: therefore came his father out, and entreated him. 29 And he answering said to father, Lo, these many years I serve thee, neither transgressed I at any time thy commandment, and yet thou never gavest me a kid, that I might be merry with my friends: 30 But as soon as this thy son was come, which hath devoured thy living with harlots, thou hast killed for him the fatted calf. 31 And he said unto him, Son, thou art ever with me, and all that I have is thine. 32 It was meet that we should make merry, and be glad: for this thy brother was dead, and is alive again; and was lost, and is found.

16:1 There was a certain rich man, which had a steward; and the same was accused unto him that he had wasted his goods. 2 And he called him, and said unto him, How is it that I hear this of thee? give account of thy stewardship; for thou mayest be no longer steward. 3 Then the steward said within himself, What shall I do? for my lord taketh away from me the stewardship: I cannot dig; to beg I am ashamed. 4 I am resolved what to do, that, when I am put out of the stewardship; they may receive me into their houses. 5 So he called every one of his lord's debtors, and said unto the first, How much owest thou unto my lord? 6 And he said, A hundred measures of oil. And he said unto him, Take thy bill, and sit down quickly, and write fifty. 7 Then said he to another, And how much owest thou? And he said, A hundred measures of wheat. And he said unto him, Take thy bill, and write fourscore. 8 And the lord commended the unjust steward, because he had done wisely: for the children of this world are in their generation wiser than the children of light. 9 And **I** say unto you, Make to yourselves friends of mammon of unrighteousness; that, when ye fail, they may receive you in everlasting habitations. 10 He that is faithful in that which is least is faithful also in much, and he that is unjust in the least is unjust also in much. 11 If therefore ye have not been faithful in the unrighteous mammon, who will commit to your trust the true? 12 And if ye have not been faithful in that which is another man's, who shall give you that which is your own? 13 No servant can serve two masters: for either he will hate the one, and love the other; or else he will hold to the one, and despise the other. Ye cannot serve **GOD** and mammon.

16:15 Ye are they which justify yourselves before men; but **GOD** knoweth your hearts: for that which is highly esteemed among men is abomination in the sight of **GOD**. 16 The law and the prophets until John: since that time the **Kingdom of GOD** is preached, and every man presseth into it. 17 And it is easier for Heaven and Earth to pass, than one little tittle of the **LAW** to fail. 18 Whosoever putteth away his wife, and marrieth another, committeth adultery: and whosoever marrieth her that is put away from husband committeth adultery. 19 There was a certain rich man, which was clothed in purple and fine linen, and fared sumptuously every day: 20 And there was a certain beggar named Lazarus, which was laid at his gate, full of sores, 21 And desiring to be fed with the crumbs which fell from the rich man's table: moreover the dogs came and licked his sores. 22 And it came to pass, that the beggar died, and was carried by the angels into Abraham's bosom: the rich man also died, and was buried; 23 And in hell he lifted up his eyes, being in torments, and seeth Abraham afar off, and Lazarus in his bosom. 24 And he cried and said, Father Abraham, have mercy on me, and send Lazarus, that he may dip the tip of his finger in water, and cool my tongue; for I am tormented in this flame. 25 But Abraham said, Son, remember that thou in thy lifetime receivedst thy good things: and likewise Lazarus evil things: but now he is comforted, and thou art tormented. 26 And beside all this, between us and you there is a great gulf fixed: so that they which would pass from hence to you cannot; neither can they pass to us, that from thence. 27 Then he said, I pray thee therefore, father, that thou wouldest send him to my father's house: 28 For I have five brethren; that he may testify unto them, lest they also come into this place of torment. 29 Abraham said unto him, They have Moses and the prophets; let them hear them. 30 And he said, Nay, Father Abraham: but if one went unto them from the dead, they will repent. 31 And he said unto him, If they hear not Moses and the prophets, neither will they be persuaded, though one rose from the dead.

17:1 It is impossible but that offenses will come: but woe, through whom they come! 2 It were better for him that a millstone were hanged from his neck, and he cast into the sea, than that he should offend one of these little ones. 3 Take heed to yourselves: If thy brother trespass against thee, rebuke him; and if he repent forgive him. 4 And if he trespass against thee seven times in a day, and seven times in a day turn again to thee saying, I repent; thou shalt forgive him.

17:6 If ye had faith as a grain of mustard seed, ye might say to this sycamine tree, Be thou plucked up by the root, and be thou planted in the sea: and it should obey you. 7 But which of you, having a servant plowing or feeding cattle, will say unto him by and by, when he is come from the field, Go and sit down to meat? 8 And will not rather say unto him, Make ready wherewith I may sup, and gird thyself, and serve me, till I have eaten and drunken; and afterward thou shalt eat and drink? 9 Doth he thank that servant because he did the things that were commanded him? I trow not. 10 So likewise ye, when ye shall have done all those things which are commanded you, say, We are unprofitable servants: we have done that which was our duty to do.

17:14 Go show yourselves unto the priests.

17:17 Were there not ten cleansed? but where the nine? 18 There are not found that returned to give **GLORY** to **GOD**, save this stranger. 19 Arise, go thy way: thy faith hath made thee whole. 20 The **Kingdom of GOD** cometh not with observation! 21 Neither shall they say, Lo here! or, lo there! for, behold, the **Kingdom of GOD** is within you. 22 The days will come, when you will desire to see one of the days of the **SON of MAN**, and ye shall not see. 23 And they shall say to you, See here; or, see there: go not after, nor follow. 24 For as lightning, that lighteneth out of the one under Heaven, shineth unto the other under Heaven; so shall the **SON of MAN** be in **HIS** day. 25 But first must **HE** suffer many things, and be rejected of this generation. 26 And as it was in the days of Noe, so shall it be also in the days of the **SON of MAN**. 27 They did eat, they drank, they married wives, they were given in marriage, until the day that Noe entered into the ark, and the flood came, and destroyed them all. 28 Likewise also as it was in the days of Lot; they did eat, they drank, they brought, they sold, they planted, they builded: 29 But the same day that Lot went out of Sodom it rained fire and brimstone from Heaven and destroyed all. 30 Even thus shall it be in the day when the **SON of MAN** is revealed. 31 In that day, he which shall be on the housetop, and his stuff in the house, let him not come down to take it away: and he that is in the field, let him likewise not return back. 32 Remember Lot's wife. 33 Whosoever shall seek to save his life shall lose it; and whosoever shall lose his life shall preserve it. 34 **I** tell you, in that night there shall be two in one bed; the one shall be taken, and the other shall be left. 35 Two shall be grinding together; the one shall be taken, and the other left. 36 Two shall be in the field; the one shall be taken, and the other left. 37 Wheresoever the body, thither will the eagles gathered together.

18:2 There was in a city a judge, which feared not **GOD**, neither regarded man: 3 And there was a widow in that city; and she came unto him, saying, Avenge me of mine adversary. 4 And he would not for a while: but afterward he said within himself, Though I fear not **GOD**, nor regard man; 5 Yet because this woman troubleth me, I will avenge her, lest by her continual coming she weary me. 6 Hear what the unjust judge saith. 7 And shall not **GOD** avenge **HIS** own elect, which cry day and night unto **HIM**, though **HE** bear long with them? 8 **I** tell you that **HE** will avenge them speedily. Nevertheless, when the **SON of MAN** cometh, shall **HE** find faith on the Earth?
18:10 Two men went up into the temple to pray; the one a Pharisees, and the other a publican. 11 The Pharisees stood and prayed thus within himself, **GOD**, I thank **THEE**, that I am not as other men, extortioners, unjust, adulterers, or even as this publican. 12 I fast twice in a week, I give tithes of all that I possess. 13 And the publican, standing afar off, would not lift up so much as his eyes unto **Heaven**, but smote upon his breast, saying, **GOD** be merciful to me a sinner. 14 **I** tell you, this man went down to his house justified than the other: for every one that exalteth himself shall be abased; and he that humbleth himself shall be exalted.
18:16 Suffer little children to come unto **ME**, and forbid them not: for of such is the **Kingdom of GOD**. 17 Verily **I** say unto you, Whosoever shall not receive the **Kingdom of GOD** as a little child shall in no wise enter therein.

18:19 Why callest thou **ME** good? none good, save one, **GOD**. 20 Thou knowest the **Commandments,** Do not commit adultery, Do not kill, Do not steal, Do not bear false witness, Honor thy father and thy mother.
18:22 Yet lackest thou one thing: sell all that thou hast, and distribute unto the poor, and thou shalt have treasure in **Heaven** and come, follow **ME**.
18:24 How hardly shall they that have riches enter into the **Kingdom of GOD**! 25 For it is easier for a camel to go through a needle's eye, than for a rich man to enter into the **Kingdom of GOD**.
18:27 The things which are impossible with men are possible with **GOD**.
18:29 Verily **I** say unto you, There is no man that hath left house, or parents, or brethren, or wife, or children, for the **Kingdom of GOD's** sake, 30 Who shall not receive manifold more in this present time, and in the world to come life everlasting. 31 Behold, we go up to Jerusalem, and all things that are written by the prophets concerning the **SON of MAN** shall be accomplished. 32 For **HE** shall be delivered unto the Gentiles, and shall be mocked, and spitefully entreated, and spitted on: 33 And they shall scourge, and put **HIM** to death; and the third day **HE** shall rise again. **18:41** What wilt thou that **I** shall do unto thee? 42 Receive thy sight: thy faith hath saved thee.

19:5 Zacchaeus, make haste, and come down, for today **I** must abide at thy house.
19:9 This day is salvation come to this house, for as much as he also is a son of Abraham. 10 For the **SON of MAN** is come to seek and to save that which was lost. **19:12** A certain nobleman went into a far country to receive for himself a kingdom, and to return. 13 And he called his ten servants, and delivered them ten pounds, and said unto them, Occupy till I come. 14 But his citizens hated him, and sent a message after him, saying, We will not have this to reign over us. 15 And it came to pass, that when he was returned, having received the kingdom, then he commanded these servants to be called unto him, to whom he had given the money, that he might know how much every man had gained by trading. 16 Then came the first, saying, Lord, thy pound hath gained

ten pounds. 17 And he said unto him, Well, thou good servant: because thou hast been faithful in a very little, have thou authority over ten cities. 18 And the second came, saying, Lord, thy pound hath gained five pounds. 19 And he said likewise to him, Be thou also over five cities. 20 And another came, saying, Lord, behold, is thy pound, which I have kept laid up in a napkin: 21 For I feared thee, because thou art an austere man: thou takest up that thou layedst not down, and reapest that thou didst not sow. 22 And he saith unto him, Out of thine own mouth will I judge thee, wicked servant. Thou knewest that I was an austere man, taking up that I laid not down, and reaping that I did not sow: 23 Wherefore then gavest not thou my money into the bank, that at my coming I might have required my own with usury? 24 And he said to them that stood by, Take from him the pound, and give to him that hath ten pounds. 25 (And they said unto him, Lord, he hath ten pounds.) 26 For I say unto you, That unto every one which hath shall be given; and from him that hath not, even that he hath shall be taken away from him. 27 But these mine enemies, which would not that I should reign over them, bring hither, and slay before me.

19:30 Go ye into the village over against; in the which at your entering ye shall find a colt tied, whereon yet never a man sat: loose him, and bring. 31 And if any man ask you, Why do you loose? thus shall ye say unto him, Because the **LORD** hath need of him.

19:40 I tell you that, if these shall hold their peace, the stones would immediately cry out.

19:42 If thou hadst known, even thou, at least in this day, the things unto thy peace! but now they are hid from thine eyes. 43 For the days shall come upon thee, that thine enemies shall cast a trench about thee, and compass thee round, and keep thee in on every side, 44 And shall lay thee even with the ground, and thy children within thee; and they shall not leave in thee one stone upon another; because thou knewest not the time of thy visitation.

19:46 It is written, **MY House** is a **House of Prayer**; but ye have made it a den of thieves.

20:3 I will also ask you one thing; and answer **ME**: 4 The baptism of John, was it from **Heaven**, or of men?
20:8 Neither tell **I** you by what authority **I** do these things. 9 A certain man planted a vineyard, and let it to husbandmen, and went into a far country for a long time. 10 And at the season he sent a servant to the husbandmen, that they should give him of the fruit of the vineyard; but the husbandmen beat him, and sent him away empty. 11 And again he sent another servant: and they beat him also, and entreated him shamefully, and sent him away empty. 12 And again he sent a third: and they wounded him also, and cast out. 13 Then said the lord of the vineyard, What shall I do? I will send my beloved son: it may be they will reverence when they see him. 14 But when the husbandmen saw him, they reasoned among themselves, saying, This is the heir: come, let us kill him, that the inheritance may be ours. 15 So they cast him out of the vineyard, and killed. What therefore shall the lord of the vineyard do unto them? 16 He shall come and destroy these husbandmen, and shall give the vineyard to others. 17 What is this then that is written, The **STONE** that the builders rejected, the **SAME** is become the **HEAD of the Corner**? 18 Whosoever shall fall upon that **STONE** shall be broken; but on whomever **IT** shall fall, **IT** will grind to powder.
20:23 Why tempt ye **ME**? 24 Show **ME** a penny. Whose image and superscription hath it? 25 Render therefore unto Caesar the things which be Caesar's, and unto **GOD** the things which be **GOD's.**
20:34 The children of this world marry, and are given in marriage: 35 But they which shall be accounted worthy to obtain that world, and the resurrection from the dead, neither marry, nor are given in marriage: 36 Neither can they die any more: for they are equal unto the angels; and are the children of **GOD**, being the children of the resurrection. 37 Now that the dead are raised, even Moses showed at the bush, when he calleth the **LORD the GOD** of Abraham, and the **GOD** of Isaac, and the **GOD** of Jacob. 38 For **HE** is not a **GOD** of the dead, but of the living: for all live unto **HIM. 20:41** How say they that **CHRIST** is David's son? 42 And David himself saith in the book of Psalms, The **LORD** saith unto my **LORD**, Sit **THOU** on **MY** right hand, 43 Till I make **THINE** enemies **THY** footstool. 44 David therefore calleth **HIM LORD**, how is **HE** then his son?

The Blood of Christ

20:46 Beware of the scribes, which desire to walk in long robes, and love greetings in the markets, and the highest seats in the synagogues, and the chief rooms at feasts; 47 Which devour widow's houses, and for a show make long prayers: the same shall receive greater damnation.

21:3 Of a truth **I** say unto you, That this poor widow hath cast in more than they all: 4 For all these have of their abundance cast in unto the offerings of **GOD**: but she of her penury hast cast in all the living that she had.
21:6 These things that ye behold, the days will come, in the which there shall not be left one stone upon another, that shall not be thrown down.
21:8 Take heed that ye be not deceived: for many shall come in **MY NAME**, saying, I am; and the time draweth near: go ye not therefore after them. 9 But when ye shall hear of wars and commotions, be not terrified: for these things must first come to pass; but the end is not by and by. 10 Nation shall rise against nation, and kingdom against kingdom: 11 And great earthquakes shall be in divers places, and famines, and pestilences: and fearful sights and great signs shall there be from **Heaven**. 12 But before all these, they shall laid their hands on you, and persecute, delivering up to the synagogues, and into prisons, being brought before kings and rulers for **MY NAME's** sake. 13 And it shall turn to you for a testimony. 14 Settle therefore in your hearts, not to meditate before what ye shall answer: 15 For **I** will give you a mouth and wisdom, which all your adversaries shall not be able to gainsay or resist. 16 And ye shall be betrayed both by parents, and brethren, and kinsfolk, and friends, and of you shall they cause to be put to death. 17 And ye shall be hated of all for **MY NAME's** sake. 18 But there shall not be a hair of your head perish. 19 In your patience possess ye your souls. 20 And when ye shall see Jerusalem compassed with armies, then know that the desolation thereof is nigh. 21 Then let them which are in Judea flee to the mountains; and let them that are in the midst of it depart out; and let not them that are in the countries enter thereinto. 22 For these be the days of vengeance, that all things which are written may be fulfilled. 23 But woe unto them that are with child, and to them that give suck, in those days! for there shall be great distress in the land, and wrath upon this people. 24 And they shall fall

by the edge of the sword, and shall be led away captive into all nations: and Jerusalem shall be trodden down of the Gentiles, until the times of the Gentiles be fulfilled. 25 And there shall be signs in the sun, and in the moon, and in the stars; and upon the Earth distress of nations, with perplexity; the sea and waves roaring; 26 Men's hearts failing for fear, and for looking after those things which are coming on the Earth: for the powers of Heaven shall be shaken. 27 And then shall they see the **SON of MAN** coming in a cloud with **POWER** and great **GLORY**. 28 And when these things begin to come to pass, then look up, and lift up your heads; for your redemption draweth nigh. 29 Behold the fig tree, and all the trees; 30 When they now shoot forth, ye see and know of your own selves that summer is now nigh at hand. 31 So likewise ye, when ye see these things come to pass, know ye that the **Kingdom of GOD** is nigh at hand. 32 Verily **I** say unto you, This generation shall not pass away, till all be fulfilled. 33 Heaven and Earth shall pass away; but **MY WORDS** shall not pass away. 34 And take heed to yourselves, lest at any time your hearts be overcharged with surfeiting, and drunkenness, and cares of this life, and that day come upon you unawares. 35 For as a snare shall it come on all them that dwell on the face of the whole Earth. 36 Watch ye therefore, and pray always, that ye may be accounted worthy to escape all these things that shall come to pass, and to stand before the **SON of MAN**.

22:8 Go and prepare us the passover, that we may eat.
22:10 Behold, when ye are entered into the city, there shall a man meet you, bearing a pitcher of water; follow him into the house where he entereth in. 11 And ye shall say unto the goodman of the house, The **MASTER** saith to thee, Where is the guest chamber, where **I** shall eat the passover with **MY** disciples? 12 And he shall show you a large upper room furnished: there make ready.
22:15 With desire **I** have desired to eat this passover with you before **I** suffer: 16 For **I** say unto you, **I** will not any more eat thereof, until it be fulfilled in the **Kingdom of GOD**. 17 Take this, and divide among yourselves: 18 For **I** say unto you, **I** will not drink of the fruit of the vine; until the **Kingdom of GOD** shall come. 19 This is **MY Body** which is given for you: this do in remembrance of **ME**. 20 This cup the **New**

Testament in **MY Blood**, which is shed for you, 21 But, behold, the hand of him that betrayeth **ME** with **ME** on the table. 22 And truly the **SON of MAN** goeth, as it was determined: but woe unto that man by whom **HE** is betrayed!

22:25 The kings of the Gentiles exercise lordship over them; and they that exercise authority upon them are called benefactors. 26 But ye not so: but he that is greatest among you, let him be as the younger; and he that is chief, as he that doeth serveth. 27 For whether greater, he that sitteth at meat, or he that serveth? not he that sitteth at meat? but **I AM** among you as **HE** that serveth. 28 Ye are they which have continued with **ME** in **MY** temptations. 29 And **I** appoint unto you a Kingdom, as **MY FATHER** hath appointed unto **ME**; 30 That ye may eat and drink at **MY** table in **MY Kingdom**, and sit on thrones judging the twelve tribes of Israel. 31 Simon, Simon, behold, Satan hath desired you, that he may sift as wheat: 32 But **I** have prayed for thee, that thy faith fail not: and when thou art converted, strengthen thy brethren. **22:34 I** tell thee, Peter, the cock shall not crow this day, before that thou shalt thrice deny that thou knowest **ME**. 35 When **I** sent you without purse, and scrip, and shoes, lacked ye anything? 36 But now, he that hath a purse, let him take, and likewise scrip: and he that hath no sword, let him sell his garment, and buy one. 37 For **I** say unto you, that this that is written must yet be accomplished in **ME,** And **HE** was reckoned among the transgressors: for the things concerning **ME** have an end. 38 It is enough. **22:40** Pray that ye enter not into temptation.

22:42 FATHER, if **THOU** be willing, remove this cup from **ME,** nevertheless, not **MY WILL,** but **THINE,** be done.

22:46 Why sleep ye? Rise and pray, lest ye enter into temptation.

22:48 Judas, betrayest thou the **SON of MAN** with a kiss?

22:51 Suffer ye thus far. 52 Be ye come out, as against a thief, with swords and staves? 53 When **I** was daily with you in the temple, ye stretched forth no hands against **ME**: but this is your hour, and the power of darkness.

22:61 Before the cock crow, thou shalt deny **ME** thrice.

22:67 If **I** tell you, ye will not believe: 68 And if **I** also ask, you will not answer **ME**, nor let go. 69 Hereafter the **SON of MAN** sit on the right hand of the **POWER of GOD**. Ye say that **I AM**.

23:3 Thou sayest.

23:28 Daughters of Jerusalem, weep not for **ME**, but weep for yourselves, and for your children. 29 For, behold, the days are coming, in the which they shall say, Blessed the barren, and the wombs that never bare, and the paps which never gave suck. 30 Then shall they begin to say to the mountains, Fall on us; and to the hills, Cover us. 31 For if they do these things in a green tree, what shall be done in the dry? **23:34 FATHER**, forgive them; for they know not what they do.

23:43 Verily **I** say unto thee, Today shalt thou be with **ME** in paradise.

23:46 FATHER, into **THY** hands **I** commend **MY SPIRIT**.

24:7 The **SON of MAN** must be delivered into the hands of sinful men, and be crucified, and the third day rise again.

24:17 What manner of communications these that ye have one to another, as ye walk, and are sad?

24:19 What things?

24:25 O fools, and slow of heart to believe all that the prophets have spoken: 26 Ought not **CHRIST** to have suffered these things, and to enter into **HIS GLORY**? **24:36** Peace unto you.

24:38 Why are you troubled? and why do thoughts arise in your hearts? 39 Behold **MY** hands and **MY** feet, that it is **I MYSELF**: handle **ME**, and see; for a spirit hath not flesh and bones, as ye see **ME** have.

24:41 Have ye any meat?

24:44 These the words which **I** spake unto you, while **I** was yet with you, that all things must be fulfilled, which were written in the law of Moses, and the prophets, and the psalms, concerning **ME**.

24:46 Thus it is written, and thus it behooved **CHRIST** to suffer, and to rise from the dead the third day: 47 And that repentance and remission of sins should be preached in **HIS NAME** among all the nations, beginning at Jerusalem. 48 And ye are witnesses of these things. 49 And, behold, **I** send the **PROMISE** of **MY FATHER** upon you: but tarry ye in the city of Jerusalem, until ye be endued with **POWER** from **HIGH**.

What JESUS Said
1&2 CORINTHIANS

11:24 Take, eat; this is **MY BODY**, which is broken for you: this do in remembrance of **ME**. 25 This cup is the **New Testament** in **MY BLOOD**: this do ye, as oft as ye drink, in remembrance of **ME**.

12:9 MY GRACE is sufficient for thee: for **MY STRENGTH** is made **PERFECT** in weakness.

What JESUS Said
ACTS

The Blood of Christ

1:4 Which, ye heard of **ME**. 5 For John truly baptized with water; but ye shall be baptized with the **HOLY GHOST** not many days hence.
1:7 It is not for you to know the times or seasons, which the **FATHER** hath put in **HIS OWN POWER**. 8 But ye shall receive **POWER**, after that the **HOLY GHOST** is come upon you: and ye shall be witnesses unto **ME** both in Jerusalem, and in all Judea, and in Samaria, and unto the uttermost part of the Earth.

9:4 Saul, Saul, why persecutest thou **ME**? 5 **I AM JESUS** whom thou persecutest: hard for thee to kick against the pricks. 6 Arise, and go into the city, and it shall be told thee what thou must do.
9:10 Ananias. 11 Arise, and go into the street which is called Straight, and inquire in the house of Judas for called Saul of Tarsus: for, behold, he prayeth, 12 And hath seen a vision a man named Ananias coming in, and putting hand on him, that he might receive his sight.
9:15 Go thy way: for he is a chosen vessel unto **ME**, to bear **MY NAME** before the Gentiles, and kings, and the children of Israel: 16 For **I** will show him how great things he must suffer for **MY NAME**'s sake.

10:13 Rise, Peter; slay and eat.
10:15 What **GOD** hath cleansed, call not thou common.

11:7 Arise, Peter; slay and eat.
11:9 What **GOD** hath cleansed, call not thou common.
11:16 John indeed baptized with water; but ye shall baptized with the **HOLY GHOST**.

18:9 Be not afraid, but speak, and hold not thy peace: 10 For **I AM** with thee, and no man shall set on thee to hurt thee: for **I** have much people in this city.

20:35 It is more blessed to give than to receive.

22:7 Saul, Saul, why persecutest thou **ME**? 8 **I AM JESUS of Nazareth**, whom thou persecutest.
22:10 Arise, and go to Damascus; and there it shall be told thee of all things which are appointed for thee to do.
22:18 Make haste, and get thee quickly out of Jerusalem: for they will not receive thy testimony concerning **ME**.
22:21 Depart, for **I** will send thee far hence unto the Gentiles.

23:11 Be of good cheer, Paul: for as thou hast testified of **ME** in Jerusalem, so must thou bear witness also at Rome.

26:14 Saul, Saul, why persecutest **ME**? hard for thee to kick against the pricks. 15 **I AM JESUS** whom thou persecutest. 16 But rise, and stand upon thy feet: for **I** have appeared unto thee for this purpose, to make thee a minister and a witness both of these things which thou hast seen, and of those things in the which **I WILL** appear unto thee; 17 Delivering thee from the people, and the Gentiles, unto whom now I send thee, 18 To open their eyes, and to turn from darkness to light, and power of Satan unto **GOD**, that they may receive forgiveness of sins, and inheritance among them which are sanctified by faith that is in **ME**.

What JESUS Said

JOHN

1:38 What seek ye? 39 Come and see.
1:42 Thou art Simon the son of Jona: thou shalt be called Cephas. 43 Follow **ME**.
1:47 Behold an Israelite indeed, in whom is no guile! 48 Before that Philip called thee, when thou wast under the fig tree **I** saw thee.
1:50 Because **I** said unto thee, **I** saw thee under the fig tree, believest thou? thou shalt see greater things than these. 51 Verily, verily, **I** say unto you, Hereafter ye shall see **Heaven** open, and the angels of **GOD** ascending and descending upon the **SON of MAN**.

2:4 Woman, what have **I** to do with thee? **MINE** hour is not yet come.
2:7 Fill the waterpots with water. 8 Draw out now and bear to the governor of the feast.
2:16 Take these things hence; make not **MY FATHER'S House** a house of merchandise.
2:19 Destroy this **TEMPLE**, and in three days **I** will raise **IT** up.

3:3 Verily, verily, **I** say unto thee, Except a man be born again, he cannot see the **Kingdom of GOD.**
3:5 Verily, verily, **I** say unto thee, Except a man be born of water and the **SPIRIT**, he cannot enter into the **Kingdom of GOD.** 6 That which is born of the flesh is flesh; and that which is born of the **SPIRIT** is **SPIRIT**. 7 Marvel not that **I** said unto thee, Ye must be born again. 8 The wind bloweth where it listeth, and thou hearest the sound thereof, but canst not tell whence it cometh, and whither it goeth: so is everyone born of the **SPIRIT**.
3:10 Art thou a master of Israel, and knowest not these things? 11 Verily, verily, **I** say unto thee, We speak that we do know, and testify that we have seen; and ye receive not our witness. 12 If **I** have told you Earthly things, and ye believe not, how shall ye believe, if **I** tell you **Heavenly** things? 13 And no man hath ascended up to **Heaven**, but **HE** that came down from **Heaven**, the **SON of MAN** which is in **Heaven**. 14 And as Moses lifted up the serpent in the wilderness, even so must the **SON of MAN** be lifted up: 15 That whosoever believeth in **HIM** should not perish, but have eternal life. 16 For **GOD** so loved the

world, that **HE** gave **HIS** only begotten **SON**, that whosoever believeth in **HIM** should not perish, but have everlasting life. 17 For **GOD** sent not **HIS SON** into the world to condemn the world; but that the world through **HIM** might be saved. 18 He that believeth on **HIM** is not condemned: but he that believeth not is condemned already, because he hath not believed in the **NAME** of the only begotten **SON of GOD**. 19 And this is the condemnation, that **LIGHT** is come into the world, and men loved darkness rather than the **LIGHT**, because their deeds were evil. 20 For everyone that doeth evil hateth the **LIGHT**, neither cometh to the **LIGHT**, lest his deeds should be reproved. 21 But he that doeth truth cometh to the **LIGHT**, that his deeds may be manifest, that they are wrought in **GOD**.

4:7 Give **ME** to drink.
4:10 If thou knewest the **GIFT of GOD**, and **WHO** it is that saith to thee, Give **ME** to drink; thou wouldest have asked of **HIM**, and **HE** would have given thee **LIVING WATER**.
4:13 Whosoever drinketh of this water shall thirst again: 14 But whosoever drinketh of the **WATER** that **I** shall give him shall never thirst; but the **WATER** that **I** shall give him shall be in him a well of **WATER** springing up into everlasting life.
4:16 Go, call thy husband, and come hither. 17 Thou hast well said, I have no husband: 18 For thou hast had five husbands; and he whom thou now hast is not thy husband: in that saidst thou truly.
4:21 Woman, believe **ME**, the hour cometh, when ye shall neither in this mountain, nor in Jerusalem, worship the **FATHER**. 22 Ye worship ye know not what: we know what we worship; for salvation is of the Jews. 23 But the hour cometh, and now is, when the worshippers shall worship the **FATHER** in **SPIRIT** and in **TRUTH**: for the **FATHER** seeketh such to worship **HIM**. 24 **GOD a SPIRIT**: and they that worship **HIM** must worship in **SPIRIT** and in **TRUTH**.
4:26 I that speak unto thee **AM**.
4:32 I have meat to eat that ye know not of.
4:34 MY meat is to do the **WILL** of **HIM** that sent **ME**, and to finish **HIS WORK**. 35 Say not ye, There are yet four months, and cometh

harvest? behold, **I** say unto you, Lift up your eyes, and look on the fields; for they are white already to be harvest. 36 And he that reapeth receiveth wages, and gathereth fruit unto life eternal: that both he that soweth and he that reapeth may rejoice together. 37 And herein is that saying true, One soweth, and another reapeth. 38 **I** sent you to reap that whereon ye bestowed no labor: other men labored, and ye are entered into their labors.

4:48 Except ye see signs and wonders, ye will not believe.
4:50 Go thy way; thy son liveth.
4:53 Thy son liveth.

5:6 Wilt thou be made whole?
5:8 Rise, take up thy bed, and walk.
5:11 Take up thy bed, and walk. 12 Take up thy bed, and walk?
5:14 Behold, thou art made whole: sin no more, lest a worse thing come unto thee.
5:17 MY FATHER worketh hitherto, **I** work.
5:19 Verily, verily, **I** say unto you, The **SON** can do nothing of **HIMSELF**, but what **HE** seeth the **FATHER** do: for what things soever **HE** doeth, these also doeth the **SON** likewise. 20 For the **FATHER** loveth the **SON**, and showed **HIM** all things that **HIMSELF** doeth: and **HE** will show **HIM** greater works than these, that ye may marvel. 21 For as the **FATHER** raiseth up the dead, and quickeneth; even so the **SON** quickeneth whom **HE** will. 22 For the **FATHER** judgeth no man, but hath committed all judgement unto the **SON**: 23 That all should honor the **SON**, even as they honor the **FATHER**. He that honoreth not the **SON** honoreth not the **FATHER** which hath sent **HIM**. 24 Verily, verily, **I** say unto you, He that heareth **MY WORD**, and believeth on **HIM** that sent **ME**, hath everlasting life, and shall not come into condemnation; but is passed from death unto life. 25 Verily, verily, **I** say unto you, The hour is coming, and now is, when the dead shall hear the voice of the **SON of GOD**: and they that hear shall live. 26 For as the **FATHER** hath life in **HIMSELF**; so hath **HE** given to the **SON** to have life in **HIMSELF**; 27 And hath given **HIM** authority to execute judgement also, because **HE** is the **SON of**

MAN. 28 Marvel not at this: for the hour is coming, in the which all that are in the graves shall hear **HIS** voice, 29 And shall come forth; they that have done good, unto the resurrection of life; and they that have done evil, unto the resurrection of damnation. 30 **I** can of **MINE OWN SELF** do nothing: as **I** hear, **I** judge: and **MY** judgement is just; because **I** seek not **MINE OWN WILL**, but the **WILL** of the **FATHER** which hath sent **ME**. 31 If **I** bear witness of **MYSELF**, **MY** witness is not true. 32 There is another that beareth witness of **ME**; and **I** know that the witness which he witnesseth of **ME** is truth. 33 Ye sent to John, and he bare witness unto the **TRUTH**. 34 But **I** receive not testimony from man: but these things **I** say, that ye might be saved. 35 He was a burning and shining light: and ye were for a season to rejoice in his light. 36 But **I** have greater witness than of John: for the **WORKS** which the **FATHER** hath given **ME** to finish, the same **WORKS** that **I** do, bear witness of **ME**, that the **FATHER** hath sent **ME**. 37 And the **FATHER HIMSELF**, which hath sent **ME**, hath borne witness of **ME**. Ye have neither heard **HIS VOICE** at any time, nor seen **HIS SHAPE**. 38 And ye have not **HIS WORD** abiding in you: for **WHOM HE** hath sent, **HIM** ye believe not. 39 Search the Scriptures; for in them ye think ye have eternal life: and they are they which testify of **ME**. 40 And ye will not come to **ME**, that ye might have life. 41 **I** receive not honor from men. 42 But **I** know you, that ye have not the love of **GOD** in you. 43 **I AM** come in **MY FATHER'S NAME**, and ye receive **ME** not: if another shall come in his own name, him you will receive. 44 How can ye believe, which receive honor one of another, and seek not the honor that from **GOD** only? 45 Do not think that **I** will accuse you to the **FATHER**: there is that accuseth you, Moses, in whom ye trust. 46 For had ye believed Moses, ye would have believed **ME**: for he wrote of **ME**. 47 But if ye believe not his writings, how shall ye believe **MY WORDS**?

6:5 Whence shall we buy bread, that these may eat?
6:10 Make the men sit down.
6:12 Gather up the fragments that remain, that nothing be lost.
6:20 It is **I**; be not afraid.

6:26 Verily, verily, **I** say unto you, Ye seek **ME**, not because ye saw the miracles, but because ye did eat of the loaves, and were filled. 27 Labor not for the meat which perisheth, but for that meat which endureth unto everlasting life, which the **SON of MAN** shall give unto you: for **HIM** hath **GOD the FATHER** sealed.

6:29 This is the **WORK of GOD,** that ye believe on **HIM** whom **HE** hath sent.

6:32 Verily, verily, **I** say unto you, Moses gave you not that bread from **Heaven**; but **MY FATHER** giveth you the **TRUE BREAD** from **Heaven.** 33 For the **BREAD of GOD is HE** which cometh down from **Heaven**, and giveth life unto the world.

6:35 I AM the BREAD of LIFE: he that cometh to **ME** shall never hunger; and he that believeth on **ME** shall never thirst. 36 But **I** said unto you, That ye also have seen **ME**, and believe not. 37 All that the **FATHER** giveth **ME** shall come to **ME**; and him that cometh to **ME** **I** will in no wise cast out. 38 For **I** came down from **Heaven**, not to do **MINE OWN WILL**, but, the **WILL of HIM** that sent **ME**. 39 And this is the **FATHER's WILL** which hath sent **ME**, that of all which **HE** hath given **ME I** should lose nothing, but should raise it up again at the last day. 40 And this is the **WILL of HIM** that sent **ME**, that every one which seeth the **SON**, and believeth on **HIM**, may have everlasting life: and **I** will raise him up at the last day. 41 **I AM the BREAD** which came down from **Heaven.** 42 **I** came down from **Heaven?** 43 Murmur not among yourselves. 44 No man can come to **ME**, except the **FATHER** which hath sent **ME** draw him: and **I** will raise him up at the last day. 45 It is written in the prophets, And they shall be all taught of **GOD.** Every man therefore that hath heard, and hath learned of the **FATHER,** cometh unto **ME.** 46 Not that any man hath seen the **FATHER,** save **HE WHICH is of GOD, HE** hath seen the **FATHER.** 47 Verily, verily, **I** say unto you, He that believeth on **ME** hath everlasting life. 48 **I AM** that **BREAD of LIFE.** 49 Your fathers did eat manna in the wilderness, and are dead. 50 This is the **BREAD** which cometh down from **Heaven,** that a man may eat thereof, and not die. 51 **I AM the LIVING BREAD** which came down from **Heaven**: if any man eat of this **BREAD**, he shall live for

ever: and the **BREAD** that **I** will give is **MY FLESH**, which **I** will give for the life of the world.
6:53 Verily, verily, **I** say unto you, Except ye eat the **FLESH of the SON of MAN**, and drink **HIS BLOOD**, ye have no life in you. 54 Whoso eateth **MY FLESH**, and drinketh **MY BLOOD**, hath eternal life; and **I** will raise him up at the last day. 55 For **MY FLESH** is meat indeed, and **MY BLOOD** is drink indeed. 56 He that eateth **MY FLESH** and drinketh **MY BLOOD**, dwelleth in **ME**, and **I** in him. 57 As the **LIVING FATHER** hath sent **ME**, and **I** live by the **FATHER**; so he that eateth **ME**, even he shall live by **ME**. 58 **THIS** is that **BREAD** which came down from Heaven: not as your fathers did eat manna, and are dead: he that eateth of this **BREAD** shall live for ever. **6:61** Doth this offend you? 62 And if you see the **SON of MAN** ascend up where **HE** was before? 63 It is the **SPIRIT** that quickeneth; the flesh profiteth nothing: the **WORDS** that **I** speak unto you, are **SPIRIT**, and are **LIFE**. 64 But there are some of you that believe not. 65 Therefore said **I** unto you, that no man can come unto **ME**, except it were given unto him of **MY FATHER**.
6:67 Will ye also go away?
6:70 Have not **I** chosen you twelve, and one of you is a devil?

7:6 MY time is not yet come: but your time is always ready. 7 The world cannot hate you; but **ME** it hateth, because **I** testify of it, that the works thereof are evil. 8 Go ye up unto this feast: **I** go not up yet unto this feast; for **MY** time is not yet full come.
7:16 MY DOCTRINE is not **MINE**, but **HIS** that sent **ME**. 17 If any man will do **HIS WILL**, he shall know of the **DOCTRINE**, whether it be of **GOD**, or **I** speak of **MYSELF**. 18 He that speaketh of himself seeketh his own glory: but **HE** that seeketh **HIS GLORY** that sent **HIM**, the **SAME is TRUE**, and no unrighteousness is in **HIM**. 19 Did not Moses give you the law, and none of you keepeth the law? Why go ye about to kill **ME**?
7:21 I have done one **WORK**, and ye all marvel. 22 Moses therefore gave unto you circumcision; (not because it is of Moses, but of the fathers;) and ye on the sabbath day circumcise a man. 23 If a man on

the sabbath day receive circumcision, that the law of Moses should not be broken; are ye angry at **ME**, because **I** have made a man every whit whole on the sabbath day? 24 Judge not according to the appearance, but judge righteous judgement.
7:28 Ye both know **ME**, and ye know whence **I AM** : and **I AM** not come of **MYSELF**, but **HE** that sent **ME is TRUE**, whom ye know not. 29 But **I** know **HIM**; for **I AM** from **HIM**, and **HE** hath sent **ME**.
7:33 Yet a little while am **I** with you, and **I** go unto **HIM** that sent **ME**. 34 Ye shall seek **ME**, and shall not find: and where **I AM**, ye cannot come.
7:36 Ye shall seek **ME**, and shall not find: and where **I AM**, ye cannot come? 37 If any man thirst, let him come unto **ME**, and drink. 38 He that believeth on **ME**, as the Scripture hath said, out of his belly shall flow rivers of **LIVING WATER**.

8:7 He that is without sin among you, let him first cast a stone at her.
8:10 Woman, where are those thine accusers? hath no man condemned thee? 11 Neither do **I** condemn thee: go, and sin no more. 12 **I AM the LIGHT of the WORLD**: he that followeth **ME** shall not walk in darkness, but shall have the **LIGHT of LIFE. 8:14** Though **I** bear record of **MYSELF, MY** record is true: for **I** know whence **I** came, and whither **I** go; but you cannot tell whence **I** come, and whither **I** go. 15 Ye judge after the flesh; **I** judge no man. 16 And yet if **I** judge, **MY** judgement is true: for **I AM** not alone, but **I** and the **FATHER** that sent **ME**. 17 It is also written in your law, that the testimony of two men is true. 18 **I AM** one that bear witness of **MYSELF**, and the **FATHER** that sent **ME** beareth witness of **ME**. 19 Ye neither know **ME**, nor **MY FATHER**: if ye had known **ME**, ye should have known **MY FATHER** also.
8:21 I go **MY** way, and ye shall seek **ME**, and shall die in your sins: whither **I** go, ye cannot come. 22 Whither **I** go, ye cannot come. 23 Ye are from beneath; **I AM** from above: ye are of this world; **I AM** not of this world. 24 **I** said therefore unto you, that ye shall die in your sins: for if ye believe not that **I AM**, ye shall die in your sins. 25 Even that **I** said unto you from the beginning. 26 **I** have many things to say and to

judge you: but **HE** that sent **ME** is **TRUE**; and **I** speak to the world those things which **I** have heard of **HIM**.

8:28 When ye have lifted up the **SON of MAN**, then shall ye know that **I AM**, and **I** do nothing of **MYSELF**; but as **MY FATHER** hath taught **ME**, **I** speak these things. 29 And **HE** that sent **ME** is with **ME**: the **FATHER** hath not left **ME** alone; for **I** do always those things that please **HIM**.

8:31 If ye continue in **MY WORD**, are ye **MY** disciples indeed; 32 And ye shall know the **TRUTH**, and the **TRUTH** shall make you free. 33 Ye shall be made free? 34 Verily, verily, **I** say unto you, Whosoever committeth sin is the servant of sin. 35 And the servant abideth not in the house for ever: the **SON** abideth ever. 36 If the **SON** therefore shall make you free, ye shall be free indeed. 37 **I** know that you are Abraham's seed; but ye seek to kill **ME**, because **MY WORD** hath no place in you. 38 **I** speak that which **I** have seen with **MY FATHER**: and ye do that which ye have seen with your father. 39 If ye were Abraham's children, ye would do the works of Abraham. 40 But now ye seek to kill **ME**, a **MAN** that hath told you the **TRUTH**, which **I** have heard of **GOD**: this did not Abraham. 41 Ye do the deeds of your father. 42 If **GOD** were your **FATHER**, ye would love **ME**: for **I** proceeded forth and come from **GOD**; neither came **I** of **MYSELF**, but **HE** sent **ME**. 43 Why do ye not understand **MY** speech? because ye cannot hear **MY WORD**. 44 Ye are of father the devil, and the lusts of your father ye will do: he was a murderer from the beginning, and abode not in the **TRUTH**, because there is no truth in him. When he speaketh a lie, he speaketh of his own: for he is a liar, and the father of it. 45 And because **I** tell the **TRUTH**, ye believe **ME** not. 46 Which of you convinceth **ME** of sin? And if **I** say the **TRUTH**, why do you not believe **ME**? **47** **He** that is of **GOD** heareth **GOD's WORDS**: ye therefore hear not, because ye are not of **GOD**.

8:49 **I** have not a devil; but **I** honor **MY FATHER**, and ye do dishonor **ME**. 50 And **I** seek not **MINE own GLORY**: there is **ONE** that seeketh and judgeth. 51 Verily, verily, **I** say unto you, If a man keep **MY** saying, he shall never see death. 52 If a man keep **MY** saying, he shall never taste of death.

8:54 If I honor **MYSELF**, **MY Honor** is nothing: it is **MY FATHER** that **Honoreth ME**; of whom ye say, that **HE** is your **GOD**: 55 Yet ye have not known **HIM**; but **I** know **HIM**: and if **I** should say, **I** know **HIM** not, I should be a liar like unto you: but **I** know **HIM**, and keep **HIS Saying**. 56 Your father Abraham rejoiced to see **MY** day: and he saw, and was glad.

8:58 Verily, verily, I say unto you, Before Abraham was, **I AM**.

9:3 Neither hath this man sinned, nor his parents; but that the **WORKS of GOD** should be made manifest in him. 4 I must **WORK the WORKS of HIM** that sent **ME**, while it is day: the night cometh, when no man can work. 5 As long as **I** in the world, **I AM the LIGHT of the WORLD**.

9:7 Go wash in the pool of Siloam.

9:11 Go to the pool of Siloam, and wash.

9:35 Dost thou believe on the **SON of GOD**?

9:37 Thou hast both seen **HIM**, and it is **HE** that talketh with thee.

9:39 For judgement **I AM** come into this world, that they which see not might see; and that they which see might be made blind.

9:41 If ye were blind, ye should have no sin: but now ye say, We see, therefore your sin remaineth.

10:1 Verily, verily, I say unto you, He entereth not by the door into the sheepfold, but climbeth up some other way, the same is a thief and robber. 2 But **HE** that entereth in by the door is the **SHEPHERD** of the sheep. 3 To **HIM** the **PORTER** openeth; and the sheep hear **HIS** voice: and **HE** calleth **HIS** own sheep by name, and leadeth them out. 4 And when **HE** putteth forth **HIS** own sheep, **HE** goeth before them, and the sheep follow **HIM**; for they know **HIS** voice. 5 And a stranger will they not follow, but will flee from him: for they know not the voice of strangers.

10:7 Verily, verily, I say unto you, **I AM** the **DOOR** of the sheep. 8 All that ever came before **ME** are thieves and robbers: but the sheep did not hear them. 9 **I AM** the **DOOR**; by **ME** if any man enter in, he shall be saved, and shall go in and out, and find pasture. 10 The thief cometh not, but for to steal, and to kill, and to destroy; **I AM** come that they might have life, and they might have more abundantly. 11 **I AM** the **GOOD SHEPHERD**: the **GOOD SHEPHERD** giveth **HIS LIFE** for the sheep. 12 But he that is a hireling, and not the **SHEPHERD**, whose own the sheep are not, seeth the wolf coming, and leaveth the sheep, and fleeth: and the wolf catcheth them, and scattereth the sheep. 13 The hireling fleeth, because he is a hireling, and careth not for the sheep. 14 **I AM the GOOD SHEPHERD**, and know **MY**, and am known of **MINE**. 15 As the **FATHER** knoweth **ME**, even so know **I** the **FATHER**: and I lay down **MY LIFE** for the sheep. 16 And other sheep I have, which are not of this fold: them also I must bring, and they shall hear **MY** voice; and there shall be one fold, one **SHEPHERD**. 17 Therefore doth **MY FATHER** love **ME**, because I lay down **MY LIFE**, that I may take it again. 18 No man taketh it from **ME**, but **I** lay it down of **MYSELF**. I have **POWER** to lay it down, and I have **POWER** to take it again. This **Commandment** have I received of **MY FATHER**.

10:25 I told you, and ye believed not, the **WORKS** that I do in **MY FATHER's NAME, THEY** bear witness of **ME**. 26 But ye believe not, because ye are not of **MY** sheep, as I said unto you. 27 **MY** sheep hear **MY** voice, and I know them, and they follow **ME**: 28 And I give unto them eternal life; and they shall never perish, neither shall any pluck them out of **MY** hand. 29 **MY FATHER**, which gave **ME** is **GREATER** than all: and no is able to pluck out of **MY FATHER's** hand. 30 I and **FATHER** are **ONE**.

10:32 Many **GOOD WORKS** have I showed you from **MY FATHER**, for which of those **WORKS** do ye stone **ME**?

10:34 Is it not written in your law, I said, Ye are gods? 35 If **HE** called them gods, unto whom the **WORD of GOD** came, and the **Scriptures** cannot be broken; 36 Say ye of **HIM**, whom the **FATHER** hath sanctified, and sent into the world, Thou blasphemest; because I said, **I AM the SON of GOD**? 37 If I do not the **WORKS** of **MY FATHER**, believe **ME** not. 38 But if I do, though ye believe not **ME**, believe the **WORKS**; that ye may know, and believe, that the **FATHER** in **ME**, and I in **HIM**.

11:4 This sickness is not unto death, but for the **GLORY of GOD**, that **the SON of MAN** might be **GLORIFIED** thereby.
11:7 Let us go into Judea again.
11:9 Are there not twelve hours in a day? If any man walk in the day, he stumbleth not, because he seeth the **LIGHT of the WORLD**. 10 But if a man walk in the night, he stumbleth, because there is no light in him. 11 Our friend Lazarus sleepeth; but **I** go, that **I** may awake him out of sleep.
11:14 Lazarus is dead. 15 And **I AM** glad for your sakes that **I** was not there, to the intent ye might believe; nevertheless let us go unto him.
11:23 Thy brother shall rise again.
11:25 I AM the RESURRECTION and **the LIFE**: he that believeth in **ME**, though he were dead, yet shall he live: 26 And whosoever liveth and believeth in **ME** shall never die. Believest thou this?
11:34 Where have you laid him?
11:39 Take, ye away the stone. 40 Said **I** not unto thee, that if thou wouldest believe, thou shouldest see the **GLORY of GOD**? 41 **FATHER, I** thank **THEE** that **THOU** hast heard **ME**. 42 And **I** knew that **THOU** hearest **ME** always: but because of the people which stand by **I** said, that they may believe **THOU** hast sent **ME**. 43 Lazarus, come forth. 44 Loose him, and let him go.

12:7 Let her alone: against the day of **MY** burying hath she kept this. 8 For the poor always ye have with you; but **ME** ye have not always.
12:23 The hour is come, that the **SON of MAN** should be glorified. 24 Verily, verily, **I** say unto you, Except a corn of wheat fall into the ground and die, it abideth alone: but if it die, it bringeth forth much fruit. 25 He that loveth his life shall lose it, and he that hateth his life in this world shall keep it unto life eternal. 26 If any man serve **ME**, let him follow **ME**; and where **I AM**, there shall also **MY** servant be: if any man serve **ME**, him will **FATHER** honor. 27 Now is **MY** soul troubled; and what shall **I** say? **FATHER**, save **ME** from this hour: but for this cause came **I** unto this hour. 28 **FATHER**, glorify **THY NAME**.
12:30 This **VOICE** came not because of **ME**, but for your sakes. 31 Now is the judgement of this world: now shall the prince of this world

be cast out. 32 And **I**, if **I** be lifted up from the Earth, will draw all unto **ME**.

12:34 The **SON of MAN** must be lifted up. 35 Yet a little while is the **LIGHT** with you. Walk while ye have the **LIGHT** lest darkness come upon you: for he that walketh in darkness knoweth not whither he goeth. 36 While you have **LIGHT**, believe in the **LIGHT**, that ye may be the children of the **LIGHT**.

12:44 He that believeth on **ME**, believeth not on **ME**, but on **HIM** that sent **ME**. 45 And he that seeth **ME** seeth **HIM** that sent **ME**. 46 **I AM** come a **LIGHT** into the world, that whosoever believeth on **ME** should not abide in darkness. 47 And if any man hear **MY WORDS**, and believe not, **I** judge him not: for **I** came not to judge the world, but to save the world. 48 He that rejecteth **ME**, and receiveth not **MY WORDS**, hath **ONE** that judgeth him: the **WORD** that **I** have spoken, the **SAME** shall judge him in the last day. 49 For **I** have not spoken of **MYSELF**; but the **FATHER** which sent **ME**, **HE** gave **ME** a **COMMANDMENT**, what **I** should say, and what **I** should speak. 50 And **I** know that **HIS COMMANDMENT** is **LIFE EVERLASTING**: whatsoever **I** speak therefore, even as the **FATHER** said unto **ME**, so **I** speak.

13:7 What **I** do thou knowest not now; but thou shalt know hereafter. 8 If **I** wash thee not, thou hast no part with **ME**.

13:10 He that is washed needeth not save to wash feet, but is clean every whit: and ye are clean, but not all. 11 Ye are not all clean. 12 Know ye what **I** have done to you? 13 Ye call **ME MASTER** and **LORD**: and ye say well; for **I AM** . 14 If **I** then, **LORD** and **MASTER**, have washed your feet; ye also ought to wash one another's feet. 15 For **I** have given you an example, that ye should do as **I** have done to you. 16 Verily, verily, **I** say unto you, The servant is not greater than his **LORD**; neither **HE** that is sent greater than **HE** that sent **HIM**. 17 If ye know these things, happy are ye if ye do them. 18 **I** speak not of you all: **I** know whom **I** have chosen: but that the **Scripture** may be fulfilled, He that eateth bread with **ME** hath lifted up his heel against **ME**. 19 Now **I** tell you before it come, that, when it is come to pass, ye may believe that **I AM**.

20 Verily, verily, **I** say unto you; He that receiveth whomsoever **I** send receiveth **ME**; and he that receiveth **ME** receiveth **HIM** that sent **ME**. **21** Verily, verily, **I** say unto you, That one of you shall betray **ME**.
13:26 He it is, to whom **I** shall give a sop, when **I** have dipped. **27** That thou doest, do quickly.
13:31 Now is the **SON of MAN** glorified, and **GOD** is glorified in **HIM**. **32** If **GOD** be glorified in **HIM**, **GOD** shall also glorify **HIM** in **HIMSELF**, and shall straightway glorify **HIM**. **33** Little children, yet a little while **I AM** with you. Ye shall seek **ME**; and as **I** say unto the Jews, Whither **I** go, ye cannot come; so now **I** say unto you. **34** A new **COMMANDMENT I** give unto you. That ye **LOVE** one another; as **I** have **LOVED** you, that ye also love one another. **35** By this shall all know that ye are **MY** disciples, if ye have love one to another. **36** Whither **I** go, thou canst not follow **ME** now; but thou shalt follow **ME** afterward.
13:38 Wilt thou lay down thy life for **MY** sake? Verily, verily, **I** say unto thee, The cock shall not crow, till thou hast denied **ME** thrice.

14:1 Let not your heart be troubled: ye believe in **GOD**, believe also in **ME**. **2** In **MY FATHER**'s house are many mansions: if not, **I** would have told you. **I** go to prepare a place for you. **3** And if **I** go and prepare a place for you, **I** will come again, and receive you unto **MYSELF**; that where **I AM**, ye may be also. **4** And whither **I** go ye know, and the **WAY** ye know.
14:6 I AM the **WAY,** the **TRUTH,** and **the LIFE**: no man cometh unto the **FATHER**, but by **ME**. **7** If ye have known **ME**, ye should have known **MY FATHER** also: and from henceforth ye know **HIM**, and have seen **HIM**.
14:9 Have **I** been so long time with you, and yet hast thou not known **ME**, Philip? he that hath seen **ME** hath seen the **FATHER**; and how sayest thou, Show us the **FATHER**? **10** Believest thou not that **I AM** in the **FATHER**, and the **FATHER** in **ME**? the **WORDS** that **I** speak unto you **I** speak not of **MYSELF**: but the **FATHER** that dwelleth in **ME**, **HE** doeth the **WORKS**. **11** Believe **ME** that **I** in the **FATHER**, and the **FATHER** in **ME**: or believe **ME** for the very **WORKS**' sake.

12 Verily, verily, **I** say unto you, He that believeth on **ME**, the **WORKS** that **I** do shall he do also; and greater than these shall he do; because **I** go unto **MY FATHER**. 13 And whatsoever ye shall ask in **MY NAME**, that will **I** do, that the **FATHER** may be **GLORIFIED** in the **SON**. 14 If ye shall ask anything in **MY NAME**, **I** will do. 15 If ye love **ME**, keep **MY COMMANDMENTS**. 16 And **I** will pray the **FATHER**, and **HE** shall give you another **COMFORTER**, that **HE** may abide with you forever; 17 The **SPIRIT of TRUTH**; whom the world cannot receive, because it seeth **HIM** not, neither knoweth **HIM**: but ye know **HIM**; for **HE** dwelleth with you, and shall be in you. 18 **I** will not leave you comfortless: **I** will come to you. 19 Yet a little while, and the world seeth **ME** no more; but ye see **ME**: because **I** live, ye shall live also. 20 At that day ye shall know that **I** in **MY FATHER**, and ye in **ME**, and **I** in you. 21 He that hath **MY COMMANDMENTS**, and keepeth **THEM**, he it is that loveth **ME**: and he that loveth **ME** shall be loved of **MY FATHER**, and **I WILL Love** him, and will manifest **MYSELF** to him.

14:23 If a man love **ME**, he will keep **MY WORDS**: and **MY FATHER** will love him, and **WE** will come unto him, and make **OUR** abode with him. 24 He that loveth **ME** not keepeth not **MY SAYINGS** : and the **WORD** which ye hear is not **MINE**, but the **FATHER's** which sent **ME**. 25 These things have **I** spoken unto you, being present with you. 26 But the **COMFORTER, the HOLY GHOST,** whom the **FATHER** will send in **MY NAME, HE** shall teach you all things, and bring all things to your remembrance, whatsoever **I** have said unto you. 27 **PEACE I** leave with you, **MY PEACE I** give unto you: not as the world giveth, give **I** unto you. Let not your heart be troubled, neither let it be afraid. 28 Ye have heard how **I** said unto you, **I** go away, and come unto you. If ye loved **ME**, ye would rejoice, because **I** said, **I** go unto the **FATHER**: for **MY FATHER** is **GREATER** than **I**. 29 And now **I** have told you before it come to pass, that, when it is come to pass, ye might believe. 30 Hereafter **I** will not talk much with you: for the prince of this world cometh, and hath nothing in **ME**. 31 But that the world may know that **I LOVE** the **FATHER**; and as the **FATHER** gave **ME COMMANDMENT**, even so **I** do. Arise, let us go hence.

15:1 I AM the **TRUE VINE**, and **MY FATHER** is the **HUSBANDMAN**. 2 Every branch in **ME** that beareth not fruit **HE** taketh away: and every that beareth fruit, **HE** purgeth it, that it may bring forth more fruit. 3 Now ye are clean through the **WORD** which I have spoken unto you. 4 Abide in **ME**, and **I** in you. As the branch cannot bear fruit of itself, except it abide in the **VINE**; no more can ye, except ye abide in **ME**. 5 **I AM** the **VINE**, ye the branches. He that abideth in **ME**, and **I** in him, the same bringeth forth much fruit; for without **ME** ye can do nothing. 6 If a man abide not in **ME**, he is cast forth as a branch, and is withered; and men gather them, and cast into the fire, and they are burned. 7 If ye abide in **ME** and **MY WORDS** abide in you, ye shall ask what ye will, and it shall be done unto you. 8 Herein is **MY FATHER GLORIFIED,** that ye bear much fruit; so shall ye be **MY** disciples. 9 As the **FATHER** hath **LOVED ME**, so have **I LOVED** you: continue ye in **MY LOVE**. 10 If ye keep **MY COMMANDMENTS**, ye shall abide in **MY LOVE**; even as **I** have kept **MY FATHER's COMMANDMENTS**, and abide in **HIS LOVE**. 11 These things have **I** spoken unto you, that **MY JOY** might remain in you, and your joy might be full. 12 This is **MY COMMANDMENT,** That ye love one another, as **I** have **LOVED** you. 13 Greater **LOVE** hath no man than this, that a **MAN** lay down **HIS LIFE** for **HIS** friends. 14 Ye are **MY** friends, if ye do whatsoever **I COMMAND** you. 15 Henceforth **I** call you not servants: for the servant knoweth not what **HIS LORD** doeth: but **I** have called you friends; for all things that **I** have heard of **MY FATHER I** have made known unto you. 16 Ye have not chosen **ME**, but **I** have chosen you, and ordained you, that ye should go and bring forth fruit, and your fruit should remain; that whatsoever ye shall ask of the **FATHER** in **MY NAME, HE** may give it you. 17 These things **I COMMAND** you, that ye love one another. 18 If the world hate you, ye know that it hated **ME** before you. 19 If ye were of the world, the world would love his own; but because ye are not of the world, but **I** have chosen you out of the world, therefore the world hateth you. 20 Remember the **WORD** that **I** said unto you, The servant is not greater than his **LORD**. If they have persecuted **ME**, they will also persecute you: if they have kept **MY SAYING,** they will keep yours also. 21 But all these things will they do unto you for **MY NAME's** sake, because they know not **HIM** that sent **ME**. 22 If **I** had not come and spoken unto them, they had not had sin; but now they have no cloak for their sin. 23 He that hateth **ME** hateth **MY FATHER** also. 24 If **I** had not done among them the **WORKS** which none other man did, they had not had sin: but now have they both seen and hated both **ME** and **MY FATHER**. 25 But, that the **WORD** might be fulfilled that is written in their law, They hated **ME** without a cause. 26 But when the **COMFORTER** is come, whom **I** will send unto you from the **FATHER**, the **SPIRIT of TRUTH**, which proceedeth from the **FATHER**, **HE** shall testify of **ME**: 27 And ye also shall bear witness, because ye have been with **ME** from the beginning.

16:1 These things have **I** spoken unto you, that ye should not be offended. 2 They shall put you out of the synagogues: yea, the time cometh, that whosoever killeth you will think that he doeth **GOD** service. 3 And these things will they do unto you, because they have not known the **FATHER**, nor **ME**. 4 But these things have **I** told you, that when the time shall come, ye may remember that **I** told you of them. And these things **I** said not unto you at the beginning, because **I** was with you. 5 But now **I** go **MY** way to **HIM** that sent **ME**; and none of you asketh **ME**, Whither goest **THOU**? 6 But because **I** have said these things unto you, sorrow hath filled your heart. 7 Nevertheless **I** tell you the **TRUTH**; It is expedient for you that **I** go away: for if **I** go not away, the **COMFORTER** will not come unto you; but if **I** depart, **I** will send **HIM** unto you. 8 And when **HE** is come, **HE** will reprove the world of sin, and of righteousness, and of judgement: 9 Of sin, because they believe not on **ME**; 10 Of righteousness, because **I** go to **MY FATHER**, and ye see **ME** no more; 11 Of judgement, because the prince of this world is judged. 12 **I** have yet many things to say unto you, but ye cannot bear them now. 13 Howbeit when **HE**, the **SPIRIT of TRUTH**, is come, **HE** will guide you into all **TRUTH**: for **HE** shall not speak of **HIMSELF**; but whatsoever **HE** shall hear, shall **HE** speak; and **HE** will show you things to come. 14 **HE** shall **GLORIFY ME**: for **HE** shall receive of **MINE**: therefore said **I**, that **HE** shall take of **MINE**, and show unto you. 15 All things that the **FATHER** hath are **MINE**: therefore said **I** that **HE** shall take of **MINE**, and shall show unto you. 16 A little while, and ye shall not see **ME**: and again, a little while, and ye shall see **ME**, because **I** go to the **FATHER**. 17 A little while, and ye shall not see **ME**: and again a little while, and ye shall see **ME**: and, Because **I** go to the **FATHER**? 18 A little while: 19 Do ye inquire among yourselves of that **I** said, A little while, and ye shall not see **ME**: and again, a little while, and ye shall see **ME**? 20 Verily, verily, **I** say unto you, That ye shall weep and lament, but the world shall rejoice; and ye shall be sorrowful, but your sorrow shall be turned into **JOY**. 21 A woman when she is in travail hath sorrow, because her hour is come: but as soon as she is delievered of child, she remembereth no more the anguish, for joy that a man is born into the world. 22 And ye now therefore have sorrow: but **I** will see you again, and your heart shall rejoice, and your **JOY** no man taketh from you. 23 And in that day ye shall ask **ME** nothing. Verily, verily, **I** say unto you, Whatsoever ye shall ask the **FATHER** in **MY NAME**, **HE** will give you. 24 Hitherto have ye asked nothing in **MY NAME**: ask, and ye shall receive, that your **JOY** may be full. 25 These things have **I** spoken unto you in proverbs, but **I** shall show you plainly of the **FATHER**. 26 At that day ye shall ask in **My NAME**: and **I** say not unto you, that **I** will pray the **FATHER** for you: 27 For the **FATHER HIMSELF** loveth you, because ye have loved **ME**, and have believed that **I** came out from **GOD**. 28 **I** came forth from the **FATHER**, and am come into the world; again, **I** leave the world, and go to the **FATHER**.

16:31 Do ye now believe? 32 Behold, the hour cometh, yea, is now come, that ye shall scattered, every man to his own, and shall leave **ME** alone, and yet **I AM** not alone, because the **FATHER** is with **ME**. 33 These things **I** have spoken unto you, that in **ME** ye might have **PEACE**. In the world ye shall have tribulation: but be of good cheer; **I** have overcome the world.

17:1 FATHER, the hour is come; **GLORIFY THY SON**, that **THY SON** may also **GLORIFY THEE**: 2 As **THOU** hast given **HIM POWER** over all flesh, that **HE** should give eternal life to as many as **THOU** hast given **HIM**. 3 And this is life eternal, that they might know **THEE** the only **TRUE GOD**, and **JESUS CHRIST, WHOM**

THOU hast sent. 4 **I** have **Glorified THEE** on Earth: **I** have finished the **WORK** which **THOU** gavest **ME** to do. 5 And now, O **FATHER**, **GLORIFY THOU ME** with **THINE** own **SELF** with the **GLORY** which **I** had with **THEE** before the world was. 6 **I** have manifested **THY NAME** unto the men which **THOU** gavest **ME** out of the world: **THINE** they were, and **THOU** gavest them **ME**; and they have kept **THY WORD**. 7 Now they have known that all things whatsoever **THOU** hast given **ME** are of **THEE**. 8 For **I** have given unto them the **WORDS** which **THOU** gavest **ME**: and they have received, and have known surely that **I** came out from **THEE**, and they have believed that **THOU** didst send **ME**. 9 **I** pray for them: **I** pray not for the world, but for them which **THOU** hast given **ME**; for they are **THINE**. 10 And all **MINE** are **THINE**, and **THINE** are **MINE**; and **I AM** glorified in them. 11 And now **I AM** no more in the world, but these are in the world, and **I** come to **THEE, HOLY FATHER**, keep through **THINE** own **NAME** those whom **THOU** hast given **ME**, that they may be one, as **WE**. 12 While **I** was with them in the world, **I** kept them in **THY NAME** : those that **THOU** gavest **ME**. **I** have kept, and none of them is lost, but the son of perdition that the **Scripture** might be fulfilled. 13 And now come **I** to **THEE**; and these things **I** speak in the world, that they might have **MY JOY** fulfilled in themselves. 14 **I** have given them **THY WORD**; and the world hath hated them, because they are not of the world, even as **I AM** not of the world. 15 **I** pray not that **THOU** shouldest take them out of the world, but that **THOU** shouldest keep them from the evil. 16 They are not of the world, even as **I AM** not of the world. 17 Sanctify them through **THY TRUTH**: **THY WORD** is **TRUTH**. 18 As **THOU** hast sent **ME** into the world, even so have **I** also sent them into the world. 19 And for their sakes **I** sanctify **MYSELF**, that they also might be sanctified through the **TRUTH**. 20 Neither pray **I** for these alone, but for them also which shall believe on **ME** through their word; 21 That they all may be one; as **THOU, FATHER**, in **ME**, and **I** in **THEE**, that they also may be one in **US**: that the world may believe that **THOU** hast sent **ME**. 22 And the **GLORY** which **THOU** gavest **ME I** have given them; that they may be one; even as **WE** are **ONE**: 23 **I** in them, and **THOU** in **ME**, that they may be made perfect in one; and that the world may know that **THOU** hast sent **ME**, and hast **LOVED** them, as **THOU** hast **LOVED ME**. 24 **FATHER, I** will that they also, whom **THOU** hast given **ME**, be with **ME** where **I AM**; that they may behold **MY GLORY**, which **THOU** hast given **ME**: for **THOU LOVEST ME** before the foundation of the world. 25 O **RIGHTEOUS FATHER**, the world hath not known **THEE**: but **I** have known **THEE**, and these have known that **THOU** hast sent **ME**. 26 And **I** have declared unto them **THY NAME**, and will declare; that the **LOVE** wherewith **THOU** hast **LOVED ME** may be in them, and **I** in them.

18:4 Whom seek ye? 5 **I AM**. 6 **I AM**, 7 Whom seek ye? 8 **I** have told you that **I AM**: if therefore ye seek **ME**, let these go their way! 9 Of them which **THOU** gavest **ME** have **I** lost none.
18:11 Put up thy sword into the sheath: the cup which **MY FATHER** hath given **ME**, shall **I** not drink it?
18:20 I spake openly to the world; **I** ever taught in the synagogue; and in the temple, whither the Jews always resort; and in secret have **I** said nothing. 21 Why askest thou **ME**? Ask them which heard **ME**, what **I** have said unto them: behold, they know what **I** said.
18:23 If **I** have spoken evil, bear witness of the evil: but if well, why smitest thou **ME**?
18:34 Sayest thou this thing of thyself or did others tell it thee of **ME**?
18:36 MY Kingdom is not of this world! If **MY Kingdom** were of this world, then would **MY** servants fight, that **I** should not be delivered to the Jews: but now is **MY Kingdom** not from hence. 37 Thou sayest that **I AM** a **KING**. To this end was **I** born, and for this cause came **I** into the world, that **I** should bear witness unto the **TRUTH**. Everyone that is of the **TRUTH** heareth **MY VOICE**.

19:11 Thou couldest have no power against **ME**, except it were given thee from above: therefore he that delivered **ME** unto thee hath the greater sin.
19:26 Woman, behold thy son! 27 Behold, thy mother! 28 **I** thirst.
19:30 It is finished:

20:15 Woman, why weepest thou? **WHOM** seekest thou? 16 Mary. 17 Touch **ME** not; for **I AM** not yet ascended to **MY FATHER**: but go to **MY** brethren, and said unto them, **I** ascend unto **MY FATHER**, and your **FATHER**; and **MY GOD**, and your **GOD**. **20:19 PEACE** unto you.

20:21 PEACE unto you: as **FATHER** hast sent **ME**, even so send **I** you. 22 Receive ye the **HOLY SPIRIT**: 23 Whosoever sins ye remit, they are remitted unto them; whosoever ye retain, they are retained.

20:26 PEACE unto you. 27 Reach hither thy finger, and behold **MY** hands; and reach hither thy hand, and thrust into **MY** side; and be not faithless, but believing.

20:29 Thomas, because thou hast seen **ME**, thou hast believed: blessed they that have not seen, and have believed.

21:5 Children, have ye any meat? 6 Cast the net on the right side of the ship, and ye shall find.

21:10 Bring of the fish which ye have now caught.

21:12 Come dine.

21:15 Simon, of Jona, lovest **ME** more than these? Feed **MY** lambs. 16 Simon, of Jona, lovest thou **ME**? Feed **MY** sheep. 17 Simon, of Jonah, lovest thou **ME**? Lovest thou **ME**? Feed **MY** sheep. 18 Verily, verily, **I** say unto thee, When thou wast young, thou girdedst thyself, and walkest whither thou wouldest: but when thou shalt be old, thou shalt stretch forth thy hands, and another shall gird thee, and carry whither thou wouldest not. 19 Follow **ME**.

21:22 If **I** will that he tarry till **I** come, what to thee? follow thou **ME**. 23 If **I** will that he tarry till **I** come, what to thee?

What JESUS Said
REVELATION

The Blood of Christ

1:8 I AM ALPHA and **OMEGA**, the **BEGINNING** and the **ENDING, WHICH IS,** and **WHICH WAS,** and **WHICH IS TO COME, the ALMIGHTY.**
1:11 I AM ALPHA and **OMEGA**, the **FIRST** and the **LAST**: and, What thou seest, write in a book, and send unto the seven churches which are in Asia; unto Ephesus, and unto Smyrna, and unto Pergamos, and unto Thyatira, and unto Sardis, and unto Philadelphia, and unto Laodicea.
1:17 Fear not; **I AM** the **FIRST** and the **LAST**: 18 **HE** that liveth, and was dead; and, behold, **I AM** alive forevermore, **AMEN**; and have the keys of hell and of death. 19 Write the things which thou hast seen, and the things which are, and the things which shall be hereafter; 20 The mystery of the seven stars which thou sawest in **MY** right hand, and the seven golden candlesticks. The seven stars are the angels of the seven churches: and the seven candlesticks which thou sawest are the seven churches.

2:1 Unto the angel of the church of Ephesus write; These things saith **HE** that holdeth the seven stars in **HIS** right hand, **WHO** walketh in the midst of the seven golden candlesticks; 2 **I** know thy works, and thy labor, and thy patience, and how thou canst not bear them which are evil: and thou hast tried them which say they are apostles, and are not, and hast found them liars: 3 And hast borne, and hast patience, and for **MY NAME**'s sake hast labored, and hast not fainted. 4 Nevertheless **I** have against thee, because thou hast left thy **FIRST LOVE.** 5 Remember therefore from whence thou art fallen, and repent, and do the first works; or else **I** will come unto thee quickly, and remove thy candlestick out of his place, except thou repent. 6 But this thou hast, that thou hatest the deeds of the Nicolaitans, which **I** hate. 7 He that hath an ear, let him hear what the **SPIRIT** saith unto the churches; To him that overcometh will **I** give to eat of the **TREE of LIFE**, which is in the midst of the paradise of **GOD.** 8 And unto the angel of the church in Smyrna write; These things saith **the FIRST and the LAST, WHICH was dead, and is alive**; 9 **I** know thy works, and tribulation, and poverty, (but thou art rich) and the blasphemy of them which say they are Jews, and are not, but the synagogue of Satan. 10 Fear none of those things which thou shalt suffer: behold, the devil shall cast of you into prison, that ye may be tried; and ye shall have tribulation ten days: be thou faithful unto death, and **I** will give thee a crown of life. 11 He that hath an ear, let him hear what the **SPIRIT** saith unto the churches; He that overcometh shall not be hurt of the second death. 12 And to the angel of the church of Pergamos write; These things saith **HE WHICH hath the sharp sword with two edges**; 13 **I** know thy works, and where thou dwellest, where Satan's seat: and thou holdest fast **MY NAME**, and hast not denied **MY FAITH**, even in those days wherein Antipas **MY** faithful martyr, who was slain among you, where Satan dwelleth. 14 But **I** have a few things against thee, because thou hast there them that hold the doctrine of Balaam, who taught Balak to cast a stumbling block before the children of Israel, to eat things sacrificed unto idols, and to commit fornication. 15 So hast thou also them that hold the doctrine of the Nicolaitans, which **I** hate. 16 Repent; or else **I** will come unto thee quickly, and will fight against them with the **SWORD of MY Mouth**. 17 He that hath an ear, let him hear what the **SPIRIT** saith unto the churches; To him that overcometh will **I** give to eat of the hidden **MANNA**, and will give him a white **STONE**, and in the **STONE** a new **NAME** written, which no man knoweth saving he that receiveth. 18 And unto the angel of the church in Thyatira write; These things saith **the SON of GOD, WHO hath HIS eyes like unto a flame of fire, and HIS feet like fine brass**; 19 **I** know thy works, and charity, and service, and faith, and thy patience, and thy works; and the last more than the first. 20 Notwithstanding **I** have a few things against thee, because thou sufferest that woman Jezebel, which calleth herself a prophetess, to teach and seduce **MY** servants to commit fornication, and to eat things sacrificed unto idols. 21 And **I** gave her space to repent of her fornication; and she repented not. 22 Behold, **I** will cast her into a bed, and them that commit adultery with her into great tribulation, except they repent of their deeds. 23 And **I** will kill her children with death; and all the churches shall know that **I AM HE** which searcheth the reins and hearts: and **I** will give unto every one of you according to your works. 24 But unto you **I** say, and unto the rest in Thyatira, as many as have not this doctrine, and which have not known the depths of Satan, as they speak; **I** will put upon you none other burden. 25 But that which ye have, hold fast till **I** come. 26 And he that overcometh, and keepeth **MY WORKS** unto the end, to him **I** will give **POWER** over the nations: 27 And he shall rule them with a rod of iron; as the vessels of a potter shall they be broken to shivers: even as **I** received of **MY FATHER**. 28 And **I** will give him the **MORNING STAR**. 29 He that hath an ear, let him hear what the **SPIRIT** saith unto the churches.

3:1 And unto the angel of the church in Sardis write; These things saith **HE that hath the seven SPIRITS of GOD, and the seven stars**; I know thy works, that thou hast a name that thou livest, and art dead. 2 Be watchful, and strengthen the things which remain, that are ready to die: for **I** have not found thy works perfect before **GOD**. 3 Remember therefore how thou hast received and heard, and hold fast, and repent. If therefore thou shalt not watch, **I** will come on thee as a thief, and thou shalt not know what hour **I** will come upon thee. 4 Thou hast a few names even in Sardis which have not defiled their garments; and they shall walk with **ME** in white: for they are worthy. 5 He that overcometh, the same shall be clothed in white raiment; and **I** will not blot out his name out of the **BOOK of LIFE**, but **I** will confess his name before **MY FATHER**, and before **HIS** angels. 6 He that hath an ear, let him hear what the **SPIRIT** saith unto the churches. 7 And unto the angel of the church in Philadelphia write; These things saith **HE that is HOLY, HE that is TRUE, HE THAT HATH THE KEY of David, HE THAT OPENETH, AND NO MAN SHUTTETH; AND SHUTTETH; AND NO MAN OPENETH**; 8 I know thy works: behold, **I** have set before thee an open door, and no man can shut it: for thou hast little strength, and hast kept **MY WORD**, and hast not denied **MY NAME**. 9 Behold, **I** will make them of the synagogue of Satan, which say they are Jews, and are not, but do lie; behold, **I** will make them to come and worship before thy feet, and to know that **I** have **LOVED** thee. 10 Because thou hast kept the **WORD of MY PATIENCE**, I also will keep thee from the hour of temptation, which shall come upon the world, to try them that dwell upon the Earth. 11 Behold, **I** come quickly: hold that fast which thou hast, that no man take thy crown. 12 Him that overcometh will **I** make a pillar in the temple of **MY GOD**, and shall go no more out: and **I** will write upon him the **NAME of MY GOD**, and the **NAME of**

the **CITY of MY GOD, NEW JERUSALEM,** which cometh down out of Heaven from **MY GOD**: and **MY NEW NAME.** 13 He that hath an ear, let him hear what the **SPIRIT** saith unto the churches. 14 And unto the angel of the church in Laodiceans write; these things saith **the AMEN, the FAITHFUL AND TRUE WITNESS, the BEGINNING of the CREATION of GOD**; 15 I know thy works, that thou art neither cold nor hot, **I** would thou wert cold or hot. 16 So then because thou art lukewarm, and neither cold nor hot, **I** will spew thee out of **MY** mouth. 17 Because thou sayest, I am rich, and increased with goods, and have need of nothing; and knowest not that thou art wretched, and miserable, and poor, and blind, and naked: 18 **I** counsel thee to buy of **ME** gold tried in the fire, that thou mayest be rich; and white raiment, that thou mayest be clothed, and the shame of thy nakedness do not appear; and anoint thy eye with eyesalve, that thou mayest see. 19 As many as **I LOVE, I** rebuke and chasten: be zealous therefore, and repent. 20 Behold, **I** stand at the door, and knock: if any man hear **MY VOICE**, and open the door, **I** will come in to him, and will sup with him, and he with **ME.** 21 To him that overcometh will **I** grant to sit with **ME** in **MY** throne, even as **I** also overcame, and am set down with **MY FATHER** in **HIS** throne. 22 He that hath an ear, let him hear what the **SPIRIT** saith unto the churches. Come up hither, and **I** will show thee things which must be hereafter.

16:15 Behold, **I** come as a thief. Blessed he that watcheth, and keepeth his garments, lest he walk naked, and they see his shame.

22:7 Behold, **I** come quickly: blessed he that keepeth the **Sayings of the Prophecy of this BOOK.**
22:12 And, behold, **I** come quickly; and **MY** reward with **ME**, to give every man according as his work shall be. 13 **I AM ALPHA and OMEGA, the BEGINNING and the END, the FIRST and the LAST.**
22:16 I JESUS have sent **MINE** angel to testify unto you these things in the churches. **I AM the ROOT and the OFFSPRING of David, the BRIGHT and MORNINGSTAR.**
22:20 Surely **I** come quickly:

What JESUS Said about...

Abiding Jn.15:4-10 pg 84
Ability Mt. 25:14,15 pg 26
Abode Jn. 14:23 pg 83
Abstinence Lk. 21:34 pg 63
Abundant life Jn. 10:10 pg 80
Access (GOD) Jn. 10:7,9 pg 80
Accountability Lk. 12:47, 48 pg 54
Accusation Mt. 5:11 pg 5
Adultery Mt. 5:27,28 pg 6
Adversity Lk. 24:46 pg 65
Affliction Mt. 24:7-12 pg 24
Agreement Mt. 18:19 pg 18
Ambition Lk. 22:25-30 pg 64
Anger Mt. 5:22 pg 5
Apostasy Mt. 13:18-22 pg 14
Lk. 8:13 pg 48
Appearance Mt. 6:16 pg 7
Mt. 23:27,28 pg 23
Authority Mt. 21:24 pg 21
Lk. 10:19 pg 50

Backsliding Lk. 9:62 pg 49
Baptism Mt. 28:19 pg 29
Ac. 1:5 pg 70
Begging Lk. 16:3 pg 57,58
Beneficence Mt. 5:42 pg 6
Betrayal Mt. 26:21 pg 28
Bigotry Lk. 18:9-14 pg 60
Blasphemy Mt. 12:31,32 pg 12
Blessings Mt. 5:3-11 pg 5
Blind guides Mt. 15:14 pg 15
Borrowing Mt. 5:42 pg 6
Brothers Mt. 23:8 pg 23
Burdens Lk. 11:46 pg 52
Burials Mt. 8:22 pg 9

Call (GOD) Mt. 20:16 pg 20
Death Lk. 9:22 pg 49
Called ones Mt. 22:14 pg 22
Care (GOD) Mt. 6:30,33 pg 7
Caution Mk. 4:24 pg 33
Celibacy Mt. 19:11,12 pg 19
Charity Lk. 12:33 pg 53
Cheating Mk. 10:19 pg 37
Circumcision Jn. 15:3 pg 84
Coin Mt. 22:19-21 pg 22
Coldness Mt. 24:12 pg 24
Communication Lk. 24:17 pg 65
Compassion Mt. 15:32 pg 16
Lk. 10:33 pg 50
Compromise Mt. 5:25,26 pg 6
Conceit Lk. 18:10-12 pg 60
Conduct Mt. 5:16 pg 5
Confessing (CHRIST) Mt. 10:32,33 pg 10
Confession Lk. 18:13,14 pg 59
Confidence. Mk. 10:24 pg 37
Conflict Mt. 10:34-36 pg 10
Conscience Jn. 8:7 pg 78
Contention Mt. 18:15-17 pg 18
Contentment Jn. 6:43 pg 77
Conversion Mt. 13:15 pg 14
Corruption Lk. 11:39 pg 52
Courage Mt. 9:22 pg 9
Covenant Mk. 14:24 pg 41
Coveting Mk. 7:21,22 pg 35
Cross bearing Mt. 10:38 pg 11
Crucifixion Lk. 9:22 pg 49

Dancing Lk. 15:25-27 pg 57
Darkness Lk. 11:35 pg 52
Day Jn. 11:9 pg 81

113

Deaf Mt. 13:13-15 pg 13,14
    Example Jn. 13:15 pg 82
    Jn. 8:51 pg 79
Debts Mt. 18:24 pg 18
Deceivers Mt. 24:4,5 pg 24
Decision Mt. 6:24 pg 7
Defilement Mt. 15:11,18,19
    pg 15,16
Devil Mt. 13:38,39 pg 14
Diligence Jn. 9:4 pg 80
Disbelief Jn. 5:38 pg 76
Discernment Mt.16:2,3 pg 16
Discipleship Lk. 14:33 pg 56
Disputes Mk. 9:33 pg 36
Distress Lk. 21:23,25 pg 63
Divorce Mt. 5:31,32 pg 6
Doctrine Mk. 7:7 pg 35
Doubt Mt. 21:21 pg 21
Drunkard Lk. 7:34 pg 47
Drunkenness Lk. 21:34 pg 63
Dullness Mt. 13:13 pg 13
Duty Lk. 17:10 pg 59
Dwelling place Jn. 14:2,3 pg 83

Earth Mt. 5:18 pg 5
Earthquakes Mk. 13:8 pg 39
Economy Jn. 6:12 pg 77
Elect Mt. 24:24,31 pg 25
Election Mt. 25:34 pg 27
Employer Mt. 20:1-16 pg 19,20
Encouragement Mt. 9:2 pg 9
Endowments Mt. 25:14,15 pg 26
Endurance Mt. 10:22 pg 10
    Lk. 21:19 pg 63
Enemies Mt. 5:43,44 pg 6
Eternal life Mt. 19:29 pg 19

Eternal sin Mk. 3:29 pg 33
Etiquette Lk. 10:8 pg 50
Evil Mt. 15:19 pg 16
Exaltation Mt. 23:12 pg 23
    Godlessness Jn. 5:42,44 pg 76
Excuses Lk. 14:18-20 pg 56
Extravagance Lk. 15:11-14 pg 57

Faith Mt. 6:25 pg 7
    Mk. 11:22 pg 33
    Lk. 7:50 pg 48
Faithfulness Mt. 25:21 pg 26
Faithlessness Mt. 25:24-30
    pg 26,27
False prophets Mt. 24:71 pg 24
False witness Mt. 19:18 pg 19
Farm Mt. 22:2-6 pg 22
Fasting Mt. 6:16-18 pg 7
Faults Mt. 18:15 pg 18
Fear (GOD) Mt. 10:28 pg 10
Feast Lk. 14:8 pg 55
Feet washing Jn. 13:12-15 pg 82
Fellowship Mt. 8:11 pg 9
Flattery Lk. 6:26 pg 46
Flesh Jn. 6:53 pg 77
Flock Mt. 26:31 pg 28
Following Mt. 10:37,38 pg 11
Food Mt. 6:11,25 pg 7
    Jn. 6:27 pg 77
Fool Mt. 5:22 pg 5
Formalism Mt. 23:23-28 pg 23
Forsaking all Lk. 14:13 pg 55
Friends Lk. 11:5-8 pg 51
Frugality Jn. 6:12 pg 77
Fruitfulness Mt. 13:23 pg 14
Fruitlessness Lk. 13:6-9 pg 54,55

Generosity Mt. 25:34-40 pg 27
Gentleness Mt.5:5 pg 5
Giving Lk. 6:38 pg 46
Gladness Lk.15:32 pg 57
Glorifying(GOD) Mt. 5:16 pg 5
Gluttony Lk. 21:34 pg 63
GOD Mt.19:17,26 pg 19
    Jn. 11:25,26 pg 81
Golden rule Mt. 7:12 pg 8
Gospel Lk. 4:18 pg 45
Grace 2Cor. 12:9 pg 68
Greatness Mt. 5:19 pg 5
Grumble Jn. 6:43 pg 77
Guidance Jn. 16:13 pg 85

Happiness Mt. 5:42 pg 5
    Jn. 13:16,17 pg 82
Harlots Mt. 21:13 pg 21
Hatred Jn. 15:18,19 pg 84
Healing Mt. 10:7,8 pg 10
    Mk. 2:17 pg 32
Heart Mt. 13:19 pg 14
Heaven Lk. 16:17 pg 58
    Jn. 3:13 pg 74
Hell Mt. 5:22 pg 5
    Mt. 10:28 pg 10
Helper Jn.14:16 pg 83
    Jn.15:26 pg 85
Helpless Jn. 6:44 pg 77
Hireling Jn. 10:11-13 pg 80
HOLY SPIRIT Jn. 14:26
    pg 83,84
Home Mk. 5:19 pg 34
Honesty Mk. 10:19 pg 37
    Lk. 8:15 pg 48
Honor Mt. 6:2 pg 6
    Mt. 15:3-6 pg 15
Hospitality Lk. 14:12-14 pg 56
Humility Mt. 11:29 pg 12
    Jn. 13:14 pg 82
Hunger Mt. 5:6 pg 5
Hypocrisy Mt. 6:5 pg 6
    Lk. 6:42 pg 47

Ignorance Mt. 22:29 pg 22
Immorality Mt. 5:45 pg 6
    Mt. 25:46 pg 26,27
    Leaven Mt. 16:6 pg 16
Inconsistency Mt. 7:3-5 pg 8
    Lk. 6:41,42 pg 47
Indecision Lk. 9:62 pg 49
Indifference Mt. 24:12 pg 24
Infidelity Jn. 3:18 pg 74
Influence Mt. 5:13 pg 5
Ingratitude Lk. 17:17,18 pg 59
Innocence Mt. 10:16 pg 10
Insincerity Lk. 16:15 pg 58
Inspiration Lk. 12:12 pg 53
Instability Mt. 7:26,27 pg 8
Instructions Jn. 6:45 pg 77
Insufficiency Mk. 10:21 pg 37
Integrity Lk. 16:10 pg 58
Intercession Jn. 17:9 pg 86
Investment Mt. 6:19,20 pg 7

Jealousy Lk. 15:25-30 pg 57
Joy Mt. 25:21 pg 26
    Lk. 15:7,10 pg 56,57
Judge Mt. 7:1,2 pg 8
Judgement Mt. 11:24 pg 11,12
Judgement day Mt. 25:31-46
    pg 27

Justice Jn. 5:30 pg 76
Justification,self Lk. 16:15 pg 58

Killing Mt. 5:21,22 pg 5
Kindness Lk. 10:30-35 pg 50
Kingdom Lk. 7:28 pg 47
    Jn. 18:36 pg 87
Kiss Lk. 7:45 pg 48
Knowledge Jn. 8:31,32 pg 79

Labor Mt. 20:1-14 pg 20
Laughter Lk. 6:21 pg 46
Law Lk. 16:16 pg 58
Lawsuit Mt. 5:25,40 pg 6
Lawyer Lk.11:46 pg 52
    Offering Mt. 5:25 pg 6
    Lk. 13:20,21 pg 55
Lending Lk. 6:34,35 pg 46
Levite Lk. 10:30-32 pg 50
Liars Jn. 8:44,45 pg 79
Liberality Lk. 6:30,38 pg 46
Liberty Lk. 4:18 pg 45
Life Mt. 6:25 pg 7
    Jn. 5:40 pg 76
Light Lk. 11:33 pg 52
    Jn. 8:12 pg 78
Living water Jn. 4:10 pg 75
Loneliness Jn. 16:32 pg 8
LORD's supper Mt. 26:26-29
    pg 28
Loss, soul Mt.16:25,26 pg 16,17
Love Mt. 22:37-40 pg 22
Luke warmness Mt. 26:40,41
    pg 28
Lust Mk. 4:18,19 pg 33

Mammon Mt. 6:24 pg 7
Marriage Mt.19:4-6 pg 19
Mk. 12:25 pg 39
Martyrdom Jn. 16:1-3 pg 85
Memorial Mt. 26:13 pg 27
Mercy Mt. 5:7 pg 5
    Lk. 16:24 pg 58
Minister Lk. 10:2 pg 50
Miracles Mt. 12:28 pg 12
Mother Mt. 10:37 pg 11
Murder Mt. 15:19 pg 16
Mysteries Mt. 13:11 pg 13

Narrow way Mt. 7:13,14 pg 8
Neglect Lk. 12:47 pg 54
Neighbor Mt. 19:19 pg 19
Neutrality Mt. 12:30 pg 12
New birth Jn. 3:3,5-8 pg 74

Oath Mt. 5:33-37 pg 6
Obedience Mt. 12:50 pg 13
    Regeneration Mt. 19:28
    pg 19
Offerings Lk. 21:3,4 pg 62
Opportunity Mt. 5:25 pg 6

Paradise Lk. 23:43 pg 65
Pardoning Lk. 6:37 pg 46
Parents Mt. 10:21 pg 10
Patriotism Mt. 22:21 pg 22
Peacemakers Mt. 5:9 pg 5
Penitence Lk. 18:13 pg 60
Perception Jn. 8:43 pg 79
Perfection Mt. 5:48 pg 6
Persecution Mt. 24:9 pg 24
Perseverance Mt. 10:22 pg 10

Pharisaism Mt. 23:2-33 pg 24
Pharisees Mt. 5:20 pg 5
    Lk. 18:10-14 pg 60
Philanthropy Lk. 11:41 pg 52
Physician Mt. 9:12 pg 9
Piety Jn. 1:47 pg 74
Pleasing, GOD Jn. 8:29 pg 79
Pleasure Lk. 8:44 pg 48
Poison Mk. 16:17,18 pg 42
Polygamy Mt. 19:8,9 pg 19
Poor Mk. 14:7 pg 40
Prayer Mt. 6:9-13 pg 7
    Mt. 7:7-11 pg 8
Preaching Mk. 16:15,16 pg 42
Procrastination Mt. 25:3 pg 26
Prophets Mt. 7:15 pg 8
    Mt. 10:41 pg 11
Protection Lk. 18:3 pg 60
Providence Mt. 6:25-33 pg 7
Purity Mt. 5:8 pg 5

Ransom Mt. 20:28 pg 20
Reaping Jn. 4:35-38 pg 75
Receiving Mk. 9:37 pg 36
Reconciliation Mt. 5:23,24
    pg 5,6
    Secrecy Lk.12:2,3 pg 52
Rejecting Jn. 3:18 pg 74
Rejoicing Lk. 10:20 pg 50
Release Lk. 4:18 pg 45
Religion Mt. 25:34-36 pg 27
    Mk. 7:6-8 pg 34,35
Repentance Mt. 11:21 pg 11
    Lk. 13:28 pg 55
Reproof Mt. 11:21-23 pg 11
Resignation Mt. 26:39 pg 28

Responsibility Lk. 12:47,48 pg 54
Rest Mt. 11:28-30 pg 12
    Mt. 26:45 pg 28
Resurrection Jn. 6:40 pg 77
Retaliation Mt. 5:39-44 pg 6
Retribution Mt. 23:34,35 pg 24
Reward Mt. 10:42 pg 11
Riches Mk. 4:19 pg 33
Righteousness Mt. 5:6,20 pg 5
    Jn. 16:10 pg 85
Robbers Lk. 10:30 pg 50
    Jn. 10:1 pg 80
Robbery Mt. 23:25 pg 23

Sabbath Mt. 12:5-8 pg 12
Sackcloth Mt. 11:21 pg 11
Sacrifice Mt. 12:7 pg 12
Sacrilege Mt. 21:13 pg 21
Salt Mt. 5:13 pg 5
    Mk. 9:50 pg 37
Salvation Lk. 19:19 pg 61
    Jn. 4:22 pg 75
Samaritan Lk. 10:30-35 pg 50
Sanctification Jn. 17:17 pg 86
Satan Mt. 4:10 pg 5
    Mk. 4:15 pg 33
Scripture Mt. 21:42 pg 21.
    Lk. 4:21 pg 45
Speech Jn. 8:43 pg 79
Security Lk. 6:47,48 pg 47
Seduction Mk. 13:22 pg 40
Seeking Mt. 6:19,20 pg 7
Self-condemnation Mt. 23:29-32
    pg 24
Self-control Mt. 5:21 pg 5

Self-deception Lk. 12:16-21 pg 53
Self-denial Mt. 16:24-26 pg 16,17
Self-exaltation Mt. 23:12 pg 23
Self-examination Mt. 7:3-5 pg 8
Selfishness Lk. 6:32-35 pg 46
Self-righteousness Mt. 23:23-27 pg 23
Serpents Mt. 23:33 pg 24
   Jn. 3:14 pg 74
Service Lk. 22:27 pg 64
Sheep Lk. 15:4-7 pg 56
Shepherd Jn. 10:1-18 pg 80
Sickness Mt. 10:8 pg 10
Signs Lk. 11:16 pg 51
   Jn. 4:48 pg 75
Silence Mt. 17:9 pg 17
Sin Mt. 26:28 pg 28
   Jn. 8:34 pg 79
Sincerity Mt. 5:13-16 pg 5
Skepticism Jn. 20:27,29 pg 88
Slaves Mt. 18:23 pg 18
   Jn. 15:15 pg 84
Sleep Mk. 4:26,27 pg 33,34
   Mk. 13:35,36 pg 40
Slothfulness Mt. 25:26-30 pg 26,27
SON of MAN Lk. 9:22 pg 49
Sorrow Mt. 19:22 pg 19
   Jn. 16:6 pg 85
Soul Mt. 10:28 pg 10
   Lk. 12:19,20 pg 53
Souls winner Mt. 4:19 pg 5
Sowing Mk. 4:14 pg 33
   Vision Mt. 17:9 pg 17

Spirit Mt. 26:41 pg 28
   Mk. 5:8 pg 34
Steadfastness Mt. 10:22 pg 10
Stealing Mt. 19:18 pg 19
Steward Lk. 12:42,43 pg 54
   Lk. 16:1-8 pg 57,58
Stewardship Lk. 19:13-27 pg 61
Stomach Mt. 15:17 pg 16
Stubbornness Jn. 5:40 pg 76
Stumbling block Mt. 23:13 pg 23
Submission Mt. 26:39,42 pg 28
Suffering Mt. 26:38 pg 28
Supper, LORD Lk. 22:15-20 pg 64
Swearing Mt. 23:16-22 pg 23

Talents Mt. 18:24 pg 18
Taxes Mt. 22:19-21 pg 22
Teaching Mt. 28:19,20 pg 29
   Jn. 13:13-15 pg 82
Temperance Lk. 21:34 pg 63
Temptation Mt. 4:1-11 pg 5
   Lk. 8:13 pg 48
Thieves Mt. 6:19 pg 7
   Jn. 10:1-8 pg 80
Timidness Mk. 4:40 pg 34
Tithes Lk. 18:11,12 pg 60
Tradition Mk. 7:9,13 pg 35
Treasures Mt. 6:19-21 pg 7
Tribulations Mt. 24:9 pg 24
   Jn. 16:33 pg 86
Truth Jn. 14:6 pg 83

Unbelievers Lk. 12:46 pg 54
Uncleanness Mt. 23:27 pg 23
Unity Jn. 17:20,21 pg 86,87

Unpardonable sin Mt. 12:31, 32 pg 12
Vengeance Mt. 5:39,40 pg 6
Vine Jn. 15:1,4,5 pg 84

Walk,life Jn. 8:12 pg 78
　Jn. 12:35 pg 82
War Mt. 24:26 pg 25
Watchfulness Mt. 24:42,44 pg 25
　Lk. 12:37-40 pg 53,54
Wedding Lk. 14:8-10 pg 55
Widow Mk. 12:43,44 pg 39
Wine Lk. 5:37-39 pg 46
Wisdom Lk. 21:15 pg 63

Witness Jn. 8:14 pg 78
　False Mt. 19:18 pg 19
Witnessing Ac. 1:8 pg. 70
Wives Lk. 14:20,26 pg 56
Worker Mt. 10:10 pg 10
Worldliness Lk. 21:34 pg 63
Worm Mk. 9:43-48 pg 36,37
Worries Mt. 13:22 pg 14
Worship Mt. 4:10 pg 5

Yoke Mt. 11:28,29 pg 12

www.ingramcontent.com/pod-product-compliance
Lightning Source LLC
Chambersburg PA
CBHW060403080526
44583CB00012B/447